A Foxfire
Christmas

Contents

Primary responsibility for editing the final manuscript for A Foxfire Christmas *was taken on by a group of mostly tenth- and eleventh-graders, pictured here with a working draft. Front row, L–R: Amy Nichols, Keri Gragg, Holli Hickox, Robbie Bailey, Chuck Clay, Scott Cannon, Tammi English, Rabun Baldwin, Anthony Queen, and Rob Stockton. Back Row: Bruce Beck, Scott Crane, John Crane, Renai Crane, Caney English, Jenny Lincoln, Dale Trusty, Anna Lee, and Leigh Ann Smith. Not pictured: Roger Little.* PHOTO BY AL EDWARDS

Preface

Like the other nine books in the Doubleday Foxfire series, this one was put together by students in two of my English classes at the Rabun County High School, located in the Appalachian Mountains of northeast Georgia. And like the previous books, this one was put together in a rather unusual way. For one thing, most of the photographs were taken and printed by students who had never touched a camera before or seen the inside of a darkroom. Interviews with elderly mountain residents were conducted and edited by students who had never before interviewed anyone, transcribed tapes, or written a single word for purposes of publication. Like the other Foxfire books, in other words, this one was created by young people who didn't know how.

Beyond that fact, there are several aspects that make this volume unique from even the Foxfire series itself.

First, it was created in two completely distinct and separate phases and thus it has two student-written introductions. The sixty-four-page Doubleday Christmas card, described in Kelly's introduction, was produced in 1986, and then, several years later, this expanded version of that card was prepared for the general public. Each version was completed in only ten weeks. Instruction, collection, and creation was done in a whirlwind of activity that pushed all involved to the limits of their abilities.

Second, students from other Appalachian public elementary and secondary schools were invited to help us, and as the student credit section shows, about one third of this book is made up of their contributions.

Third, a former student, Al Edwards, pitched in to lift from my shoulders the bulk of the instruction in photography and printing—the first time a former student has been so directly and responsibly involved in a project of this sort.

Fourth, the manuscript was prepared on Macintosh equipment, and rather than using contract labor, as in the past, to type the final manuscript, the students typed it all. Now, in our classroom, conversion to the new technology is almost complete. Once we get that scanner . . .

Fifth, unlike the other books in the Foxfire series, an unprecedented amount of the material collected never made it into print. Some 80 percent had to be rejected because of repetition—how many versions of "all we got was an orange and a stick of candy" can one use?—all in the interests of sharing with you the very essence of what was collected, not the bulk. In many cases, out of thirty or forty pages of interview transcript, only one three-sentence gem made it into this volume—a tough but valuable lesson for students going into print for the first time.

Sixth, material that appeared in the Foxfire series usually was printed in our quarterly magazine, *Foxfire*, first, but the students who collected it rarely saw it printed in book form until long after they had graduated from our high school. In some cases, the time lapse was as much as seven or eight years. This time, nearly seventy students who worked on the manuscript for this book will have finished copies in their hands before they graduate. Many will enclose copies with their applications to college, and I'll be amazed if that doesn't help their chances for admission.

In some ways, the creation of a book manuscript by strangers to the process is a perversion of conventional wisdom. In the teaching profession, however, analogies are plentiful. Under competent, sometimes skillful, instruction, a ragtag group of novices is brought together and molded into a school orchestra, a dramatic troupe, a football team, a choral ensemble, a debate group, or a roomful of inventors or researchers or draftsmen or scientific experimenters or artists. In fact, the creation of something of substance by people who have never done it before is not a contradiction but, in teaching, is precisely the point. It is the highest form of our craft.

And thousands of anonymous public school teachers manage to do it every single day. In part, it's what you pay us for.

—Eliot Wigginton

Kelly's Introduction

❄ Christmas Day, 1915. A new snow has fallen overnight outside a one-room hand-built log cabin tucked into a
valley somewhere in the hills of the Appalachian Mountains. Roosters crow as the rising sun slowly spreads its
light across the white ground, and the family inside begins
to stir. The six children in the loft have been awake for
hours whispering about Santa Claus and quietly laughing
over the tricks they played on their neighbors while "serenading" the night before. They can hardly contain their
excitement as they anxiously await the sound of their father grinding the morning coffee—their cue to get up.

Below, their simple stockings dangle from the fireplace mantel, each heavy with the weight of three apples, two oranges, stick candy, and the traditional Brazil nut wedged in the toe. Santa Claus has been good to them this year. When these treasures have been found and the morning chores done, the children will spend their morning outside playing in the snow while their mother and father prepare for the traditional Christmas dinner. The salted pork that has been in the smokehouse since October will finally be brought out, and the sorghum that was put up in stoneware jars late last summer will come off the shelf to flavor the cakes for dessert.

After dinner, the family will gather around the fireplace to talk, laugh, and pray. The younger ones will silently fall asleep as their father pulls out his old wooden fiddle. Night falls as the music drifts out of the house, and Christmas is over.

There are almost as many traditions in the mountains as there are people. This typical Christmas scene is only one of the many we came across this spring after Diana Klemin asked us to create Doubleday's 1985 Christmas card. Diana was the art director at Doubleday who supervised the design of the covers of the first Foxfire books, and she has been a longtime friend of Foxfire.

When her request was received, many of the students were busy trying to meet the deadline for the next issue of *Foxfire* magazine, and others were finishing *Foxfire 9*. Still, the sound of *A Foxfire Christmas* sparked our interest, and the class voted unanimously to go ahead.

Faced with the task of going on completely new interviews to find answers to Diana's request for stories about "the small, pleasant delights of Christmas—the simple gift for each child or the one gift for the entire family, the hymns sung, the Christmas dinner, the going to church, the events of the day (tending the farm animals, completion of the usual round of chores, etc.)," we got busy immediately. In less than two weeks, we went on almost twenty interviews and transcribed and edited close to forty-five hours of tape. In the process, we discovered Christmas traditions and stories. Some told us jokes that were played on neighbors and friends during the season while others described family dinners and favorite gifts. But few neglected to mention the simplicity of their earlier Christmases. Talking to these people helped us discover a little more about ourselves and the meaning of the season.

Spring, 1985. As a junior in high school, I wrote the preceding piece to serve as an introduction to *A Foxfire Christmas*, a sixty-four-page greeting card sent out to all the friends and patrons of Doubleday. The end product was to consist only of ten interviews, forcing us to leave out many of our favorite pieces and allowing this newly discovered wealth of information to remain untapped. Of all the work I did during my five years as a Foxfire student, this simple little book was my favorite. And so it felt good to hear from Jenny Lincoln, a current Foxfire student, in the fall of 1989, informing me that the card was to be expanded into a full-length, hardcover book available to the general public.

Jenny asked for my help in the project, and so I went back home one Friday for the weekend. Now a senior in college, I had not walked into the old Foxfire classroom for three years, and I was not prepared for the greeting I received. Everything looked just as I'd remembered, except so much smaller. This book, as you see it now, was scattered about in various sections all across the room where students had been working at it. Wig and the staff members there greeted me warmly as the continuous sound of activity rumbled on. The Meaders' jugs were still there, lined up on the bookshelves along with various tools, quilts, and books—lots of books. And then there was Jenny, a vibrant tenth grader with big bright eyes whose energy filled the room. She was excited about the book and ready to get to work.

Fresh new voices of younger students, kids who hadn't even entered high school before I graduated, were taking the place of me and my friends. Watching Jenny and the other Foxfire students, I realized that somewhere along the line, I'd grown up. And so it is with Christmas, I think. Its memories are always the best. In this, our twenty-fifth anniversary year, a younger generation and an older generation come together to present to you the best of two traditions—Foxfire and Christmas.

—Kelly Shropshire

Jenny's Introduction

 Christmas.

What does this word mean to you? What pictures does it conjure up in your mind?

Gorgeous fir trees with glittering lights and incandescent silver and gold tinsel? Santa Claus, driving a reindeer sled with packages, going "Ho! Ho! Ho!"? Children leaping up at six o'clock on Christmas morning, rushing out and squealing with delight at what they find under the tree?

This is certainly the vision of Christmas most common in America today, but many do not realize that it is one which is by no means old or universal. Christmas today is a time of fun, festivity, and above all the spending of money. Yet many people are beginning to feel that there *must* be a deeper, truer meaning with which today's traditions have somehow lost touch.

How can we find this deeper, truer meaning? There is no one right answer for everyone, but perhaps one of the most intriguing ways to search is to examine the older Christmas traditions of some of the more distinctive cultures in our heritage as a nation. Some of the more fasci- nating Christmas traditions can be found among the people of the Appalachian mountains. This book, of course, is a compendium of these traditions, researched firsthand by students who, in many cases, interviewed their own grandparents.

When we first heard of the idea for this book, we were in the middle of a huge load of work. It was about halfway through the summer, and five of us had jobs with Foxfire. Three of us, only rising tenth graders, were working for the first time. We were concentrating on three big projects: getting out the already long-overdue spring issue of *Foxfire*, working on the summer issue, and doing the initial work on the book to celebrate our twenty-fifth anniversary year. Then we heard the news that Doubleday was interested in publishing an expanded hardcover edition of the Christmas card they had published three years earlier.

We were excited about this idea, but we failed to do much work on it until the beginning of the school year. Ever since then, however, our Foxfire I and II classes have worked continuously on this book, always afraid that we would not make the deadline.

Things have been quite hectic, especially as most of us, in addition to working on this book, are busy with all the activities of any regular high school student. There is the continual pressure on each of us to make good grades, to maintain a social life, to somehow find our own identity, and to become as mature as we can. Also, most of us are involved in a vast number of school activities, from athletics to band to cheerleading to debating to student government.

With all the demands on our time, perhaps it is a miracle that we finished the book. The experience, however, has certainly been worth it. It has expanded our horizons and given us opportunities for growth and change that we had never dreamed of before in our lives. Most important, it has brought many of us closer to that deep, true spiritual love and peace which is the true meaning of Christmas. If this book does the same for you, then it has served its purpose.

—Jenny Lincoln

ONE

Preparations and Decorations

Edited by Scott Cannon

Every year, starting as early as the first of December, wreaths, ribbons, and those bothersome blinking lights go up outside our homes to help exemplify the Christmas spirit. These are just a few examples of decorations people might see as they travel down a highway at Christmastime. But of course these are not all. In the houses they will also see candles glowing on an oak-stained mantel, sparkling silver and gold tinsel ropes draped around a Christmas tree, and of course, hanging above the fireplace, the stockings just waiting to be filled by Ole Saint Nick.

These decorations are what we go to the store and

burn our hard-earned cash on. But in this chapter most of the decorations described either are homemade, or are things one can find nestled in the woods.

Most of the people we interviewed gathered mistletoe and holly and pine. Most of them decorated their trees with chains made of homegrown popcorn, cranberries, and strips of paper cut from a Sears Roebuck catalog. This chapter also reveals, however, how ingenious some families were in making unique decorations for the home and tree: pine cones wrapped in the foil from a cigarette package, tiny wooden crosses carved of wood, and sycamore balls dipped in flour and water to turn them white. I wonder if our Christmas would be as meaningful if we used again the homemade traditions that preceded the age of colored electric lights and tinsel.

—Scott Cannon

"We used that star for years."
Margaret Bulgin

John and Margaret Bulgin are well suited for each other. Mr. Bulgin, with his impish grin, is like a mischievous little boy (he is in his early eighties) and Mrs. Bulgin, in her early seventies, is just the person to keep him out of trouble!

Margaret: My father was one of the fortunate people during the Depression years—before my teen years. I don't mean we were wealthy or anything like that, but we did have a regular income. We knew the money was coming. He had a job as a fire warden in this district for the North Carolina Forest Service.

We had the same dolls—my sister and I—year after year, but Mother made new clothes for them at Christmas. Another thing that contributed to our Christmas was the fact that my mother had a sister who never married. She took it as her Christian duty to provide packages at Christmas for all her nieces and nephews. The first yo-yo I ever saw came in a package from Aunt Louise at Christmas. She always included clothes, dresses, scarves, gloves, and things like that, but there'd be some foolishness, too. And always peanut brittle. She always sent peanut brittle. But not everybody had an Aunt Louise, and we knew we were very fortunate to have her.

When I was eleven or twelve years old, I wanted a suitcase worse than anything in the world. I had no intention of ever going anywhere. I didn't have any notion of traveling, but I wanted a suitcase, and I got one for Christmas that year. It was a nice little suitcase—black cardboard and a green lining, looked like taffeta. I bet that thing cost at *least* three or four dollars! That was what I wanted, and it was there! I just loved it! I put it up in my closet and I guess I eventually used it.

Course we didn't have any electric lights, so our Christmas trees didn't look like they do now. We were *never* allowed to use candles. They're just so tricky. And Father, being in the fire-fighting business, wasn't about to let us do that anyway. Aunt Louise provided ornaments, maybe sent some in packages to us, but we made a lot of them at home out of craft paper—mostly chains. Mother would bake gingerbread men. I remember very well a little sheep, a cookie cutout, that she made of gingerbread. We hung those on the tree. We made everything except for a few store-bought ornaments that Aunt Louise sent us. We'd make a star to go on top of the tree in school. Always before Christmas holidays, we were doing these things in school and bringing them home. I can remember when the first tin foil came out. We cut a star out of cardboard and covered it in tin foil. It still makes a pretty star. That was the first one I remember. We used that star for years.

Margaret Bulgin making a wreath of fresh greenery.

We'd kill a hog usually between Thanksgiving and Christmas—after the weather got cold and the meat wouldn't be as likely to spoil. They would save the bladders out of the hogs and blow them up like balloons and let them dry. They'd make an explosion when we jumped on them and popped them. We'd usually do that on Christmas Eve. It would be louder than the burst of a balloon. Made a noise kind of like a gunshot.

We always drew names and exchanged gifts at school. These were usually handmade gifts. I remember, though, my mother getting a Kewpie doll once. She and Al together dressed it, and that was the gift I gave to the girl whose name I drew at school. The same Christmas I got (and I still have it) a little black tin box with a lid. I got that little box full of fudge that [the mother of the girl who drew my name] had made.

My father's favorite dish was a pork roast. Usually about that time of year, we were killing hogs, so Mother would cook a pork loin roast for Christmas. I'd still rather have it than turkey. When I was growing up, we almost always had Christmas dinner at my grandmother's. She lived within walking distance from our house. Mother would cook the pork roast and bring it and all the baking she'd done, and we'd go to Grandmother's. One of my aunts lived up the road with her big family, and *they* would come down to Grandmother's, so it was bedlam there! Just a big family. Christmas was really just a time for everybody getting together.

Seeing what we got from Santa Claus [was my favorite part of Christmas]. I had a team of goats. One year [my daddy] made me a wagon and a harness for the goats. We got a sled he made, too. It'd snow and we'd get out and sleigh ride! I remember one time when I was pretty small we got a little red wagon. It was about [the same size] as wagons little children have now. I guess that was my favorite gift.

Mother used to start baking two weeks or more before Christmas. Pound cakes. Layer cakes. Fruit cakes. We didn't *dare* come in the house and stomp the floor when she had a pound cake in the oven! My favorite uncle, Noah Randolph, was a good cook! He'd always bring a cake or something when we'd get together. It would be just the family, and Grandmother and Grandfather. We'd go to their house for dinner in a buggy or a covered wagon, and we'd have a heated stone in the wagon to keep our feet warm.

"We'd go to their house for dinner in a buggy or a covered wagon, and we'd have a heated stone in the wagon to keep our feet warm."

John: When I was working for the power company, I'd go over there at night and I made my son a kiddie cart. Then two or three years later, after our kids got big enough, we bought three used bicycles from a friend. (This was when we just had two boys and a girl.) I worked on those bikes night after night up at the power company shop and put on new seats and sheepskin seat covers and new handle grips. I painted them and put a new tire on one of them. I was up there just about every other night working on those darned things!

I brought them home Christmas Eve and put them in one of the bedrooms. On Christmas morning there wasn't a whole lot for the kids, but when everybody was getting a little discouraged and kind of disappointed, I opened that door and told them to come in there. You never saw three kids go crazier! If they'd been brand new bicycles, they couldn't have been any happier.

Aunt Lola Cannon: One thing that we enjoyed as youngsters—we always had a Christmas tree at the church during the Christmas season. Most times we'd meet a day or two before Christmas to decorate the [church] house. We'd cut holly, white pine, and anything that was green, and decorate each window and each corner. To keep it from looking bare, we stood greenery up all the way to the ceiling. That took a day in our lives. But we stretched out a day. Oh, we thought we were really living it up when we could spend a whole day decorating the church for Christmas. And then we felt we must go back and clean it up afterward, and that took another whole day. Oh, we were just as busy as youngsters are now who work.

Leona Carver: At Bible school we would make candles. We always kept everything we ever made that way. We didn't make any at home. We'd melt wax at Bible school and color the wax. They'd be great big candles; I believe we would color them with food coloring. Back then, people didn't have no electricity. There were just lamps and candles.

Clyde English: When I was real little, I can't remember us having Christmas trees much. I remember the first real Christmas I went to. I was five years old, and it was at the old Tiger School. We went to that Christmas tree over there and everybody there got a sack with a stick of candy in it. I don't remember much else, but I remember that we got a stick of candy, and that was the first Christmas tree I had ever seen.

Later, the kids decorated the trees at school. We would prepare from one Christmas to the next, and you thought it would never get here. We didn't have events all year long like you do now.

[When we started decorating] at home, we put the decorations up on Christmas Eve and left them up until New Year's Day. It was a tradition, when I was little, to leave them up until New Year's. We'd always have plenty of holly. My mother would go out with us and get holly and put it over the mantelpiece, or over pictures in the house. We strung popcorn and made chains to put on our tree, once we started having one. And we used to make those paper chains, you know, where you take paper and make cutouts. I can fold paper and make pretty cutouts to go on trees. I can still make those paper dolls and angels where you cut folded paper one time, and then you can open it up.

And I made a lot of candles. The reason I've made so many candles is to teach other people how to make them. You can make sand candles by taking your sand and melting your wax and pouring it down in there, and that makes sand candles. You can also take honeycomb paper and roll it up and make a candle. I saw some honeycomb paper the other day.

Clyde English making a chain of paper angels.

Janie P. Taylor (Clyde English's daughter): We were aware of the ecology of our mountains, and I recall my elders saying not to hunt the perfect tree. So we'd find a tree that had a peculiar or odd shape. One side could be kind of flat to be put up against the wall. We didn't cut the perfect tree. Those trees were saved for timber.

We would string popcorn, but it was more of a family recreation than a necessity. We used native greenery such as holly, and we always had special holly trees located that had branches filled with berries. We used the holly and mistletoe and, a lot of times, cedar. Then the galax leaves were a source of green. They are shiny, green, and almost heart-shaped. They stay green all winter under the leaves where they are protected from the cold mountain weather. Before I was born, when there was a death in the community, the neighbors would go to the nearest area where they could find galax and make wreaths out of the leaves. There

19

were no florists, and so it was a gift of love because you had to go get the leaves and then make a beautiful wreath. So it was a meaningful source of decoration for Christmastime. My grandmother always used it.

Mary McDaries: My dad, with my elder brother Tom, would go into the forest behind our small home in the hills of Appalachia to look for the biggest and best tree.

Meanwhile, the others shelled, cleaned, and popped the popcorn we had grown in the summer just for this occasion. After it was popped, the smaller children were given the duty of stringing the simulated garland.

Now it was time to make the ornaments. Take some flour, yeast, milk, and various food coloring, all in direct proportion to one another. Shape your dough to the desired figure, then paint with food coloring for effect. Stick in the oven until desired hardness. You have made your beautiful tree ornaments without even leaving home.

Now it was time to make the bows. These came from scrap material saved when my mother had made the three girls' dresses over the year. We all helped make the tree-end bows.

Finally, after quite a while (Daddy was choosy about our Christmas trees), Daddy and Tom returned with what every year seemed like the best tree ever. Soon, my daddy and all my brothers had the tree stable and standing straight, tall and almost at attention to us kids.

Now it was finally time to decorate the tree.

First, being the littlest, I held the popcorn string at the bottom. This caught a great deal of temptation to bite into the string while the others wound it around and up to the top of the tree.

Next came our new dough ornaments, along with some which had been saved from Christmases gone by. Then some finishing touches were made, such as our newly finished bows.

The tree trimming was a special part of our Christmas when I was a little girl. It's still special to me today, but back then, it was untainted. Sometimes I wish things could be that simple today.

Hubert Hooper: Everybody in the family would go and help look for the Christmas tree each year. That was one of the big events at Christmastime. We'd get an ax, go in the woods, and cut a regular pine tree down. Then we brought it back and put it in the corner.

We made our own decorations. For example, we made popcorn balls, and we'd hang those up in the tree. My mother also usually made cookies of some kind, and she'd hang those on the tree, too. We'd go around and eat stuff off the tree. That was one of the best parts of Christmas.

We also usually decorated the house. We had pine cones, pine burrs, and white pine boughs that we broke off from the trees and put around the house. They made the house smell like pine. We didn't use anything that was artificial; it all came out of the forest.

And we put mistletoe over the door, and so everybody that came in the door would get kissed. This was the old-fashioned way of greeting people at Christmastime.

Louise Hooper: All we had was a tree, but we never did make our own popcorn decorations or anything like that because my mother kept a really clean house, and she didn't want us messing around in the kitchen much! We didn't have any lights, either. We had things that we made out of crepe paper.

Edith Cannon: Sometimes, to add a little bit more decoration to our Christmas tree, we would take Sears Roebuck catalogs and cut some strips of paper, and take flour and water and mix it up to make a paste. That's the only kind of glue we had. We'd cut those strips and glue them, and make chains.

Icie Rickman: You can take crepe paper and make a bow. We'd just make a bunch of these bows and hang them on the tree.

We'd also get all colors of crepe paper like, say, green, red, blue, and plait it. Plaiting is the same as braiding. That would make a pretty decoration for your tree. We would loop the plaited crepe paper through the tree like you do tinsel now.

Clyde Runion: Sometimes we'd take pine cones and wrap them in aluminum foil and make balls out of them. Make a rope out of popcorn. Wasn't no factory-made stuff on the trees yet. Everything they put on the tree they made it. Put little dolls and stuff on the trees. Little stars made of tin.

Rosa Bell Griffin: We would go find us a cedar and Dad would cut it down. We would spend all day trying to decorate it. My mom would make all kinds of stuff to put on it. She would make flowers out of yarn. My father

Edith Cannon making a paper chain.

would carve wood ornaments. My mother would keep my decorations from one year to the next. She would always take good care of them. She would store them in the old washhouse.

Eula Parker: We always had decorations for Christmas. There is a little black snail that lives on rocks in a creek. We picked them up and they had a little shell on them, and you could string them up and make beads out of them. We would string them and hang them up in the trees if we didn't have nothing else. We would find the empty hulls stuck on logs. I guess the little thing had moved on out of it. Then we had broom corn. It had a little thing growed over that looked like beads. It was a seed. You push your needle through it and string it up just like beads.

"The star was made from cardboard covered with chewing gum paper that was saved by all the children because there was no aluminum foil at that time."

Lela Maud Dean: As a family, we found a tree together. The decorations were made and popcorn was popped and strung. Chains were made from colored paper and placed on the tree. The star was made from cardboard covered with chewing gum paper that was saved by all the children because there was no aluminum foil at that time. Other ornaments were made, cut out, and placed on the tree. The first "bought" decorations were small candle holders which clipped on a tree branch. A small candle was placed in the holder on Christmas Eve, and they were lit. Dangerous to be sure, but I do not recall much thought given to that.

Stacy Barron: My grandmother [Vadie Barron] said the Christmas tree, which was a cedar tree, was cut by her father, James Mink. Mamaw said they took sycamore balls and dipped them in water. Then they rolled them in flour to make the tree look like snow.

Lucille Ponder: You ever notice the sycamore tree? There's little balls hangin' all over it. They hang down with a little stem, like. One year I got a bunch of those and I wrapped 'em in foil. Now, that was before we had many ornaments, you know. And then we'd cut up cigarette packs. They had foil inside them, and we'd cut stars and wrap that foil around the stars.

Lora Coggins: We'd string popcorn and string buck-berries. We'd pick the berries, let them dry out, and then the family would sit down and string them together.

Julianne Harris: We had a cedar tree every year. To decorate it, we would take Ivory soap flakes and water and beat it until it was like thick whipped cream. We would also add green and blue electric lights, green and blue glass ornaments, silver icicles, and a big silver star on top.

Bernice Williams: [After] one Christmas, we took down the tree, and Joyce [my sister] was telling the teensy bells good-bye. She hated to see it go. She cried.

TWO
Serenading

Edited by Holli Hickox and Tammi English

✳ When we thought of serenading, the first thing that came to our minds was people going from house to house singing Christmas carols. However, when we started to research the subject, we found that it was much more than we expected.

In earlier days, serenading was a time for younger people to get together and have fun. Imagine a pack of children roaming in the rigid weather on Christmas Eve with the help of the moonlight, or the flickering of a small lantern guiding them through the darkness. Everyone walking quietly to a neighbor's house ready to be sly and mischievous. All the children carrying cowbells or shotguns to make noise or surprise them. Then on a signal, the guns would be fired, and the bells would be rung to let the unexpecting neighbors know they had arrived.

Usually, then, the neighbors would invite them in and give treats to everyone such as oranges, apples, or even small toys.

In this chapter, you will find some very interesting stories about the adventures that younger people had while serenading. You will read about practical jokes like Icie Rickman blacking herself with soot, and stories about people taking wagons apart and reassembling them on roofs or in trees.

Perhaps you will be surprised as we were when we found out the old meaning of this word.

—Tammi English and Holli Hickox

"We'd get out there and shoot up in the air — serenading people."
Lawton Brooks

I had never met Lawton before and was surprised to learn that he is in his early eighties, because he has the energy and enthusiasm of a much younger man. I was also somewhat surprised to find him at home the first time I went over because during the spring and summer, Lawton spends as much time as possible working in his garden or fishing or helping out other people who live nearby. He always seems to be available to drive them to the doctor's office or to the grocery store. He was there for us, though, that day, and we had a wonderful time listening to his stories of serenading at Christmastime.

—Richard Edwards

Lawton Brooks: Back then there wasn't much Christmas, to tell you the truth, because there wasn't nothing for you to have like they is now. We didn't know what a firecracker was. Never heard tell of a firecracker. All the noise we made for Christmas—serenading people on Christmas Eve—we done with a shotgun. We'd get shotgun shells, fifty cents a box, and we'd get out there and shoot up in the air serenading people. Them shotgun barrels would get so hot, we'd have to set 'em down and wait awhile, and then start again.

Lawton Brooks.

Just gettin' out and going around, sneaking up to someone's house [was our entertainment at Christmastime. That's what we called serenading]. They didn't know nothing about it, and we'd just come up shooting, ringing bells, and making the durndest noise you ever heard. If they was in bed, they just as well to get up. They shore to God couldn't sleep! We'd just keep on making noise until they got up and gave us something to eat. They'd always invite us in and feed us. They'd have something for us to eat and sometimes give us a present or something.

Our parents would let us go out special nights to do our serenading. We'd never start out till about midnight. There'd be about twenty-five or thirty of us. The girls would join us, too, and we'd all go. We'd be sure everyone was in bed and had the lights all out. Everybody would make some kind of noise, one way or the other. You never heard such bells ringing, shooting, hollering, and beating old tin buckets and things. We had to walk and sometimes we'd go for five or six miles. The people that lived around in the settlement, they wasn't thick settled like they are here. There might be somebody lived here and it might be a half a mile out there to the next house, maybe a mile, but we'd go and just keep a-going till we gave 'em all a good round. Take us half the night to get back after we got through serenading people; we might serenade a dozen and not get back until daybreak. We'd be going all night nearly.

People in them days would have a cow and a horse, at least, in the stalls in the barn. While they were asleep that night, we'd take the horse out of one stall and put it in the cow's stall, and move the cow into the horse's stall. They'd go in there to milk the next morning—we liked to be there to watch—and there'd stand the ol' horse in the cow stall.

Boy, they could get mad! They'd throw their milk bucket down on the ground. They'd be mad enough to kill somebody, but they didn't know who done it. Us kids got a lotta kick out of that. We'd do all kinds of stuff like that. We'd move people's stuff, hide their axes or somethin' else. Whatever we could find loose, layin' out, we'd hide it. Wouldn't put it where he couldn't never find it, but he'd maybe have to hunt for two or three days.

There was one man we wanted to play a trick on, so we just took his wagon apart while he was asleep, took one piece of it at a time up on the barn, and put it all together again up there. So the next morning this man got looking for his wagon, and it was sitting astraddle on the corner of the barn, all put together and ready to go again. He didn't know what to think! He was really mad when he found his wagon on top of the barn. He had to go up there and take it down one piece at a time. We didn't tell the old man how we had tricked him for a long time, but it tickled him later when he found out.

Folks didn't care, though. Everybody else done it. Just like trick or treat here now on Halloween. It was just on that same basis—everybody done it. They'd just gather up, boys and girls, and they'd just take off. We thought if people ought to be serenaded, we'd give them a round. If anybody came in our settlement, they got serenaded whether they liked it or not. We have serenaded 'em till it made 'em so mad they'd die, nearly.

And we had gag gifts. I'd always fix up something that nobody wouldn't have. Wrap it up mighty nice and send it. Had a lot of fun with that. In fact, we done more of that than anything else.

A lot of people celebrated both Christmas and Old

Christmas—you know, the twelve days after December twenty-fifth. Some of the old people took all those days off for Christmas. Generally, everybody would get out and go places and stay with their friends and have a big time for three or four days.

They'd always have some kind of church business, and that's one thing we had to go to. They'd have singings and preachings. Everybody would come in and have a big do-up. You'd see horses and mules and cattle tied up all over the woods out around the church. I tell you, I've rid to church in a ol' ox wagon and there'd be so many on it, the ol' ox couldn't pull us up the hill. We'd get off and walk to the top of the hill and ride down.

I was a pretty good-sized boy before we ever had a Christmas tree. We always thought Santa Claus came down the durned chimney all the time, and we hung up our stockings, but we didn't put up no Christmas tree. Santa Claus would bring us all kinds of candy and oranges, things like that, but they wasn't many toys. I'd rather had a tricycle back then than to have a Cadillac today. We didn't have no little ol' toy pistols, cap busters, to play with. Didn't know what they was. All the guns that we ever had was made out of wood. Somebody would just whittle 'em out.

"I'd rather had a tricycle back then than to have a Cadillac today."

We'd get up about two o'clock Christmas morning. We was all early risers because my daddy always got us out at five o'clock in the morning. I don't care if it was pouring rain, snowing knee-deep, you come out of there every day. If it was too bad to get out in the field to work, we'd go to the barn and shuck corn, something or another around the barn—clean up. He always found us something to do. So we was used to getting up early.

Christmas day was a hunting day. All of us boys went a-huntin' that day. [Our parents] would let us have about two days at Christmas to hunt in, and I always had me about five or six good dogs. We'd get out there in them fields, and you talk about fun! Shooting and running rabbits—we had it! And they was a lot of rabbits then. Ain't no rabbits now. *Then* they was rabbits!

We always had a big Christmas dinner, all kinds of pies and things. We raised our own turkeys and all kinds of chicken, so we'd have our own turkey for Christmas dinner. I'd say coconut cake and lemon pie are my favorites at Christmas. I never get tired of those things. I'll eat 'em till they make me sick and I'll still love the dadblame things. I just love 'em.

"I'll eat 'em till they make me sick and I'll still love the dadblame things. I just love 'em."

We couldn't buy things at the store for Christmas like you can now. I have an idea that was really better. Now kids get so many toys they don't enjoy Christmas because every time they go to the store, it's Christmas. They won't get out of there till you buy them a toy. The *only* time we got a toy was at Christmas. And that was a year apart. But then, it just wasn't there to buy.

Burma Patterson: Everybody knowed each other and we just had the most fun. We didn't have "wheels," but we had our legs. We walked, serenading. We didn't ride in a car. We all wanted to be together. There wasn't nothing but just a road wide enough for one wagon or car to pass.

We'd take the cowbells off of the cows, and the boys would take real shotguns to shoot all around the house. We walked in a neighborhood and was real quiet. We'd wait till we'd get just right to the house, then go to shooting and running round the house—ringing bells, shooting, and screaming to the top of our voices.

They'd have every light off except for a little lamp. We wouldn't be running around there long till we'd see 'em strike a match and light a kerosene lamp, open the door, and say, "Y'all come in." They would have cake cut in little pieces for us, or an apple, an orange, or a piece of candy, and some of them would have something for us to drink. If we wasn't hungry, we'd take it with us.

If we didn't yell and whoop, why we'd go to singing Christmas songs—"Jingle Bells" and "Santa Claus Is Coming to Town." We'd go serenading whether it was warm, sleeting, raining, or snowing. We didn't let nothing stop us from doing that. That was our yearly thing. We enjoyed it. I think they ought to now, but with so many lights so close together, you'd know if anybody was coming. You couldn't slip up on them, unless you lived out in the country.

When we got through serenading, the boys would go out in the woods and get firewood and we'd build a big bonfire and tell tales and play "pleased or displeased" till midnight. Our parents were at home in the bed when we got in. Maybe my dad would be asleep but my mama would be awake, and she'd see that we were all there. My daddy would go with us lots of times to get to shoot the gun. Then he'd go on home and go to bed, and leave us young folks to have a big time.

And it was cold back then! A lot of times there'd be a big snow on the ground. We loved that, too. We didn't have boots. We didn't have money to buy boots. We'd put on our shoes and Mama would pull on a pair of wool socks that she'd knitted over our shoes and put our knee garters on, and couldn't no snow get in our shoes. We was warm as toast!

I wish we would have more white Christmases now. It'd seem more like Christmas for it to snow. It seems like we had more white Christmases then. I think it's more special for it to snow, myself. It feels so snug and secure and like Christmas ought to feel.

We had a really good time—an old-fashioned Christmas.

Leonard Hollifield: When we would get to a house, we would start shooting the guns, and if they came out and invited us in, we would quit and go inside and have a treat. It was the same thing as caroling today, or trick or treating, but that was the way we would do it.

It was the only time we did it, too. We didn't do it any other time. We would go on Christmas Eve and that was about it. There would be a bunch of grown-ups with us always to supervise, you know, so there wouldn't be anyone hurt. The chaperones kept us from getting in trouble. They had another rule at the time: if you heard someone coming in the distance, why you'd get out and fire your gun if you didn't want to entertain them, and that was how they would pass you—if you fired on them before they could fire on you. Daddy always heard the serenaders coming, and he'd shoot the double-barrel "POW! POW!" and then they would pass us by.

If he could kind of figure out who was doing the serenading, and if it wasn't a boisterous bunch—the ones that were going to be rowdy and such as that—why he'd let them come on in and give them an apple or an orange or something like that.

Robert Cannon: Down at Duncan Rufus Williams', they would always slip through the walkway and come on in and get the first shot. W. R. Williams and I tied a shotgun up in a tree and set a rock and everything back on it and pulled a line to it across the pathway. When they hit that, [it] would jerk that rifle, and KA-BOOM she'd go!

Robert Cannon.

Aunt Nora Garland: On Christmas Eve night, we'd all go serenading. We'd put on different old clothes, you know, and carry things to beat on and cow bells to ring. We went up to one place and the man told his wife, "Lula, just carry the bed out and give 'em some room." It was a great big room, and they cleared it out for dancing and playing games. And some of them did dance. I didn't, though. It was against my religion, but my brother would play the harmonica. They'd turn the room over to us, and we'd all play games like "Go in and out the windows." We'd be there till midnight.

We'd play tricks on people, too. One place where we went to dance and play games, they had two big horses with white faces. The boys took shoe polish and painted those horses' faces black. Those folks never said a word about it.

I remember one time in particular when we had serenaders come to our house and serenade us. We could just barely hear 'em a-talking. There was a great big pine thicket above the house, and we could hear 'em a'coming around the hill. Daddy reached up over the mantel and got his gun and went outside and shot straight up. He was so thrilled over that. He'd say, "Well, gentlemen and ladies, I've got the trick on you all! You've got the treat on me." When he shot the gun, they were supposed to treat the family, you know. Of course they didn't, and Daddy would always have plenty to treat them with. He'd always put a big barrel of apples away for Christmas—the very choicest apples we had—and peanuts and chestnuts and things like that. And Daddy would bring out biscuits and goodies, and Mother would set out everything she'd cooked: a great big stack of these apple pies out of dried apples, and a great big high stack of pumpkin custards. I'll never forget that.

Ruby Ivie: When we got old enough to go serenading, our daddy would go with us. We would walk from one house to another. Daddy would take his shotgun and shoot it while we slipped up to the house and yelled "Merry Christmas!" The people who had instruments and knew how to play would take theirs, and they'd play while everyone sang and ate.

Annie Perry: A bunch of people would gather together, and they'd have all kinds of noisemaking things, and they'd go slip in the dark and go to people's houses and get close to the house, and oh, they'd lower the boom on you. Made all kinda noise. Yes, and if you didn't get up and treat them, they'd do some kind of mischief to you.

Ruby Ivie.

They'd play like they'd be gone, and they'd come back and take off a wagon wheel and tie it in the top of a tree, and that wadn't much fun. But it was fun to them. Yes, that's what they did. But if you'd get up and give them a treat, why they'd go on about their business.

That's the way they done.

Bernice Taylor: I remember one time we went serenading and it looked like it was gonna rain when we left here, but we got all the crowd together from here plumb back over to where the road's not paved. It got to sleetin' and a-rainin', and we all stopped at Mr. Marvin's up there serenading. They had a big fire a-goin', and we rounded up around and stood and sung Christmas songs, and it was a-snowin' like everything. Mr. Marvin said it would quit directly, and to just sing on and have a good time.

Well, it finally got to getting deeper and deeper, and we had to come home in the snow about three o'clock in the morning!

Icie Rickman: [We'd do our serenading] a little bit before Christmas Eve. A lot of people shot guns, and we'd shoot firecrackers if we had them. Back then you could get firecrackers, but they was pretty scarce. My daddy would go to the grocery store [and get them]. [We would also have] those torpedoes in little round balls that you could throw down real quick and they'd just go off.

We'd black ourselves, you know, like black folks, and go in on people like that. [We'd take] soot out of the fireplace and just put it here and yonder. [We would] put an old red or blue handkerchief on [our] head. We didn't want to put too much soot on because it was too hard to get off. My brothers and sisters usually [put on soot], and some of our neighbors. We'd go here and yonder to houses. They were surprised; back then you didn't see too many black people. And it was a scare to the little children.

Billy Long: There were about twenty of us kids that would go. We stayed out one Christmas Eve all night long. I guess we were in our late teens. I remember we went to Jim McDowell's house. He didn't much want to get up. We got him out of bed, but he was slow about getting out. We got his shoes that had been sitting in the living room and started drawing the strings up and tied them up in knots down to the end of the string. He got up and he was just raring that we tied his shoestrings in knots. We got him good!

Elmer Ponder: We always shot a lot of firecrackers at Christmas time. Everybody that could get up a few cents, they bought firecrackers. An' we'd shoot and bang around with them things. And I got me an old tire pump, took it apart, and used the barrel. I'd light me a firecracker, and drop down in it, then drop me a walnut in on top of it and aim it like a gun. And boy, I could shoot a walnut outta sight.

Billy Long.

Bessie Kelly: We had hickory wood and my brothers would take the hickory coals while they were red hot and pour water on 'em and then hit 'em with the back of a pole ax or something like that, and those coals would shoot and sound just like firecrackers shooting. My brothers have done that a lot of times.

Edith Cannon: We never did serenade after twelve o'clock. My daddy and momma always said that mischief was always started mostly after twelve o'clock at night. We always had to be home by twelve.

The last time that we let our children go, they was in a group that got a little bit rowdy. There was about twenty-four or twenty-five of them. They just kept playing out there in the front yard throwing firecrackers, and this and that and the other. About the time I went to the door to invite them all in, somebody threw a cherry bomb on the porch and hit Elaine [our daughter] on the leg. So from then on our children never did go serenading.

Eula Parker: When we were young people, we used to be bad about shooting firecrackers on Christmas. To me that doesn't seem like that's celebrating Christ's birthday, but it was tradition at that time, and we didn't mean no harm. First, we'd shoot the firecrackers. That was to let them know that we [was on our way].

We always threw the firecrackers outside, away from people's houses. We was taught how not to burn people's houses down. We knowed how to use them, all except one time. My sister was in the crowd, and somebody throwed a firecracker and it exploded somehow. I don't know how it

40

happened, but a piece of it fell in her pocket, and it set her pocket on fire.

Florence Brooks: One time we got serenaded. Starting out at the yard and coming around to the edge of the house, there was a ditch dug a few feet deep from our waterpipe, and they came a-serenading, and everyone of them went *right* in the ditch. That's the last serenade I ever heard tell of. Boy, they went in the ditch headlong. They was muddy as a hog when they came out of there.

"There was a ditch dug a few feet deep for our waterpipe, and they came a-serenading, and every one of them went *right* in the ditch."

Bertha Dockins: They'd go serenading on Christmas Eve, and they'd go to a house and turn out their cattle, and pick up some of their things and hide them, and maybe it'd be a month before they'd tell the folks where they were. That was the young people—teenagers; old people didn't do that! One time they got a wagon and tied it up in a tree, and that old man never could find it. They had to go show it to him a month or so later. It was wild! But you know, they don't do that no more. They got to where they'd do so much damage. My husband told me about one time where he grew up, somebody shot under the floor, and the other one shot higher, and it went in and hit the man's bed where he lay. And they said they quit after that—people were getting too mean.

THREE

Gifts and Santa

Edited by Robbie Bailey

❄ Christmas Day. The day children dream of when they awake from a sleep that has filled their minds with the great things that Santa is going to bring them, and it finally comes true.

This chapter is about gifts that people received on Christmas. Most of the people mentioned getting the same things: oranges, apples, sticks of candy, chewing gum, and sometimes dolls for the girls and maybe a knife or slingshot for the boys. If you compare the gifts received today and the gifts back then, you have to say that people in this day and age have it lucky. Could you imagine children today waking up and finding an orange or an apple for their present? They would laugh in their parents' faces.

At the turn of the century, however, things were different. Aunt Mo and Tommy Lee Norton: "We were crazy about Christmas. We didn't get that much, but nobody else did either. We always looked forward to Christmas, and we still do. Even though we didn't get anything [when we were little], we looked forward to it."

At times, however, they got gifts that were different from the normal fare. These were the little special gifts they got that might not be much in size or weight but that meant much in love and affection. For example, a man might decide that his son would like a horse carved from wood. He works secretly for months to produce a present that is small but full of love. The son realizes this, and it makes him proud and brings a sparkle to his eye. We were lucky to find many examples of this, and I think that these kinds of gifts symbolize the contents of this book.

And when children got only an orange, even though it might last only thirty seconds to a minute, they enjoyed every last bite, and every seed they had to spit out of that orange.

Clyde Runion: "We never got nothing unless it was homemade, unless it was an apple, orange, or a piece of candy or two. Never got no big toys. I don't reckon we ever got a big toy at all. Just something you could put in a sock. We always liked [the candy and fruits] back then because it was something we didn't have every day. You'd go six months, probably, and never see an orange. When you did get one it tasted good, [and] the candy too. A nickel's worth of candy was a whole lot back then. Everybody was happy. Nobody got mad at what they got because nobody got nothing." I think that last line tells the story.

— Robbie Bailey

"Instead of Santa Claus coming down the chimney, he came down the stairs."

Minyard and Lessie Conner

When Minyard and Lessie Conner are together, one can always be sure of a good time. Their eyes flash toward each other, stories of mischief are revealed, and it is easy to tell that the sixty-five years they have spent together have been full of happiness.

The Conners have lived in Rabun County since 1935, when they had to leave their home in North Carolina in what is today part of the Smoky Mountains National Park.

As Minyard told us anecdotes of Christmases past, Lessie went through old cookbooks and recipes and spoke of her feelings about the meaning of Christmas to her. Minyard laughed his low, deep bellow and Lessie smiled quietly as they both remembered younger days.

— Joseph Fowler and Kelly Shropshire

Minyard: Mother knit our stockings from wool. We had lots of sheep and grew our own wool. It was just one of our regular stockings that we used for Christmas for Santa Claus. Sometimes we'd get candy and apples and an orange. The first orange I'd ever see'd was in my sock. I didn't know what they was. I liked it. I've liked oranges ever since.

My parents told me about old Santa Claus coming down the chimney and we had a big old chimney. Said he come down and delivered our presents into our stockings. I never did see his tracks, you know, where he had left any sign, and when I was about five or six years old, I was beginning to doubt Santa. One morning when I got up— Christmas morning—I found a gun in my stocking, one of those little old cap busters. I got that gun outta that stock-ing. It was the first one I'd ever seen, and the caps were just loose in a little box. I shot all the caps up that were in the stocking, and I got to wondering where I could get some more. We lived in a two-story house, and there was rooms upstairs, and I remembered seeing some of those caps on the steps. It looked like instead of Santa Claus coming down the chimney, he came down the stairs. I just tracked him back on up there to one of the upstairs rooms where they'd dropped some of them there caps. Right then, I was beginning to doubt old Santa Claus. I knowed he didn't come down the chimney.

I remember my daddy givin' me a sixteen-gauge shot-gun at Christmastime—the first real gun I ever had in my life. He wouldn't give it to me until I was big enough to shoot it and take care of it and wasn't afraid of it. He said, "I believe, son, you're gettin' nearly big enough to shoot that shotgun." Said, "Will you shoot it?"

I said, "Believe I will."

Across the road, there was an apple tree over there, and somebody had threw a cornstalk up in that tree. He said, "Shoot at that there cornstalk. If you can hit that cornstalk, you can kill a squirrel. BA-ROOM-AH! Way back yonder!" It kicked me pretty bad. He said, "I believe you can shoot it now."

Minyard Conner.

"Boys! I went to killing squirrels with that ol' shotgun. I was proud of that!"

Boys! I went to killing squirrels with that ol' shotgun. I was proud of that! He gave me the shotgun and a box of shells and we had squirrels to eat!

Sometimes we'd get presents at school. Somebody'd give you something, so you wanted to give them something. We gave mostly homemade candy made out of syrup. We didn't have nothing else. We'd have what they called a candy pulling—the girls and boys would. We'd get us a girl and pull candy. The more we worked it, the better it'd be. Made it harder and stiffer. I remember boiling the syrup down, and it'd turn white as we pulled on it.

Lessie: We have gotten gag gifts at the Christmas tree drawings sometimes. Minyard got a sandwich made out of a hog's nose. When they killed a hog to slaughter, they cut the old snout off and put it in between two pieces of light bread and tied it with sea grass. They did! Had it all wrapped up and in a pretty box, and he opened it and there was that old hog snout!

The first Christmas tree I ever seen was at our church. I must have been about thirteen or fourteen years old. We popped popcorn and strung that to put on the tree. We didn't have no ornaments or lights. We didn't have electricity. They drawed names for presents, and we all got presents. They was just wrapped in plain white wrapping paper and placed under the tree. We'd save the paper that things bought at the store was wrapped in and use that. Most of the presents was all homemade. They'd give a towel, or make somebody an apron or a set of pillowcases.

My mother knit my stockings out of wool, and these were the ones we hung up for Santa Claus. My stocking was longer than the boys'. We'd get apples, and there'd always be hard candy and sometimes we'd get chocolate candy. And we'd get these little bitty red cinnamon drops that'd burn your mouth, and long sticks of chewing gum wrapped in white paper. It wasn't in a pack. That's how it was with the first Christmases I remember. We didn't get toys until after we got bigger. I got a bought doll for

Lessie Conner.

Christmas when I was about ten years old, and I thought it was the prettiest thing I'd ever seen. It had real hair, and it'd open its eyes and was so beautiful! It was sticking in the top of my sock. Santa Claus brought it. That doll was it! I kept it for years and years.

[But] if I had my time to go over, I'd never teach my children that there was a Santa Claus. It's not right. You're teaching your children something that's not right, for we know there's not a Santa Claus. I'd teach them that *we* brought their presents. We should teach them to be honest and not give them gifts under false pretense.

[Another reason is that] we had nine children and my husband worked hard, and it was a hard time. My children would go over to our neighbors', and maybe some of them would have nice presents, and they'd come back and say, "Mommy, ol' Santa Claus don't like us."

I said, "Why?"

They'd tell me what the neighbors' children got from Santa Claus and they'd say, "He didn't bring us nothing pretty like that." And you know, that hurts. That learnt me right then. I seen right where I'd made my mistake. You see, as you grow older, you can see back to your taillights, but you can't see your headlights. I believe in being honest with anybody. If you ever marry and raise children, don't never teach them there's a Santa Claus. Tell them it's Christ's birthday, and they're supposed to give and get presents and love their neighbors.

"You see, as you grow older, you can see back to your taillights, but you can't see your headlights."

Bernice Williams and Burice Bradshaw: On Christmas morning, our brothers would get up around three or four o'clock in the morning, long before daylight. They always had firecrackers, and Peter would get ahold of them firecrackers and away he'd go. He'd shoot a big firecracker off first—beat the neighbors waking everybody up. You never heard such an explosion! I'm surprised Daddy let them buy such stuff, but that was what they liked.

Ida Neal: If you had been bad in the last year, you got knots tied in your stocking!

Clyde English: In our stockings there was always a Brazil nut in the toe, and we always had an orange and an apple and some candy. And the greatest delight was to pour it all out and see what we got. And then you kinda rationed it all out because you didn't want to eat it all Christmas Day.

Mary Pitts: We'd hang up our stockings and we'd get oranges and apples and nuts and some stick candy and sometimes raisins. The raisins wouldn't be in a box. They'd be on a stem that had the seeds.

When we were small, we didn't get many toys. I don't remember any bought toys. Mother made all of ours, even made the balls we played with out of yarn. [One year] my mama made me a big rag doll and dressed it, and Daddy made a little doll cradle.

Annie Perry: We always celebrated Christmas, ever since I've been big enough to remember. When night come we always went to the chimney corner, pulled our stockin's off, hung 'em up, and Santa Claus come while we was in bed asleep. Put up a dirty sock. It's just as good in a dirty sock as in a clean sock. We'd stick a stick in the chimney and hang them stockin's up on the stick, and when we woke up next morning it'd be full of apples, an orange, two or three sticks of candy.

Doris Shumate: Let me tell you about a Christmas morning I had one time. They had been havin' music. I was six or seven years old. Anyhow, my daddy and mother had went up to her aunt's. They had music up there. They left me at Granmaw's and Granpaw's. And my granpaw was mischievous, and he loved to devil me over something. Granpaw had a mousetrap set that night and he had caught a mouse. He got up and he laid that right on top of my sock. I got up and took my stockin' down and there laid that mouse right on top of it, and I throwed my stockin' and said, "Good God, Granpaw!" He's made me mad as long as I can remember. It tickles him to death.

Mrs. Lovell: I remember all our Christmases were special. My momma would set our plates on the table, and Santa Claus would come to see us in our plates. We usually got an apple, an orange, and some stick candy. That's all we had. Sometimes we would get nuts, and usually Momma would have made a rag doll or some kind of little toy for my sister and me. My dad would have made the boys a slingshot or a new wagon or a new sled that they could ride down the hill on. I think on Christmas morning would be the most special time when we got up to see what we had in our plates. [The most special gift I ever got] was a time [when] Daddy was real sick and we didn't have anything at all. The neighbors came and they brought us some toys and things they had made. If it had not been for that, we wouldn't have had any Christmas. We had a large family, and the neighbors knew our father was sick. Maybe he had had a tree fall on him or something, and he hadn't been able to get out and work. They brought us some rag dolls for the girls, and some toys for the boys. It made my mama and daddy so happy knowing we would be able to have something.

Alma Lusk: I remember one Christmas we begged Mama to hang her stocking up, and the next morning there was a great big old sweet potato in it. Ohhh! Us kids thought that was so funny!

Icie Rickman: My daddy would go and try to find a piece of timber, you know, that was kindly bowed up [to make sled runners]. Then he'd put a bed in it, floor it, and then the sides. He'd put two little nails there and put us a chair there, you know. You could either pull it, or get in it and sit and get pulled. Boy, we'd use our little [sled] till it would be just as slick as it could be. The more you use it, the slicker it will be.

"Boy, we'd use our little [sled] till it would be just as slick as it could be."

You'd steer it with that chain or rope he put on there. Like if you was going to get in at the top of that hill and come down, see you've got a rope in each hand to kindly guide it or you'd run in the ditch. If you didn't have that you'd go every which way.

My daddy [also] used to make little [wooden wagons] for us. He always made the boys one. You cut the wheels out of big logs like [my son] Claude's got out here. It wouldn't

A sled like the one Icie Rickman's father made when she was a child.

take more than about a week [to make the wagons], if he'd get at it. We'd get on there and just ride. [We would] have the best time on them little ol' wagons. All of us played, the girls, the boys. We loved that.

Icie Rickman spent many fun-filled hours as a child on a home-made, wooden-wheeled wagon like this one.

Robert Cannon: Our daddy used to make up wagons. He'd saw blocks out of trees and make little wheels. I'll tell you what we did. When Daddy caught us we didn't do it, but we'd take his axle grease and grease that spinner axle where them wheels would roll. And when we got caught, we didn't use any more of it.

[The only gifts we got] was a nickel pack of chewing gum. And I think an orange. I think that wound us up.

Leigh Ann Smith: My grandfather, Leonard Hollifield, once told me that his dad made tops for the children every Christmas. He had learned how to make them, and when he had his own kids, he made the tops for them for Christmas. Here are his directions for how to make tops:

To make a top, or jim dancer as we called it, you start off by finding the center of your spool, and you score a ring around it. Then you taper the spool on each side of the ring until you get to the center. Then you break it in half, and you run a stick through each hole until it's good and tight. You can tell when you're getting to the center when both

Leonard Hollifield can take a wooden spool and a stick and quickly whittle out two tops for his grandkids.

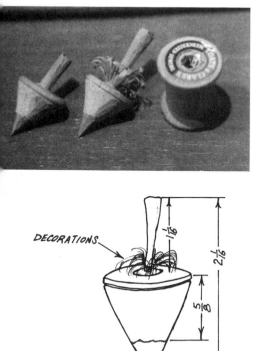

halves feel as though they are going to break apart. The last thing you have to do is trim the spool and stem together to a tapered point and cut your stem until it is how you like it.

Lora Coggins: Well, one special gift I got was a toothbrush made out of birch or black gum twigs. It was about [eight inches long], and one end was chewed to make it like a brush. We'd dip it in a snuffbox, and brush our teeth with that. We also used to use ashes out of the fireplace on our teeth. It was so special 'cause it's the first one I'd ever gotten.

Maude Brown: I made some of my gifts out of chinaberries. We'd make beads by waiting for the china-berries to ripen and fall off the tree. Then we washed them real good and boiled them to get all the pulp. They would be almost like wood. Then we dried them and put them on a string. Sometimes we painted them with pokeberries that would turn them purple.

Nicole Skeen: My grandmother [Lula Skeen] and her family had a different Christmas tradition than other fami-lies. Instead of hanging stockings, they set out big boxes with their names on them. Santa would leave them fruit, nuts, candy, and usually one toy in their boxes. She re-members her favorite gift as a little wooden pie safe that her father made for her to keep her tea set in.

Iris Patterson: I got a little tiny wicker living room suite. It consisted of a little couch, a chair, and a table with

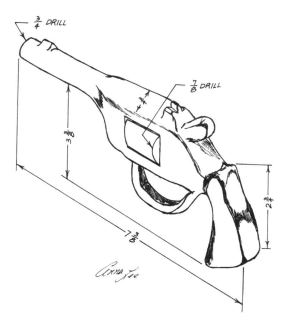

$\frac{3}{4}$ DRILL

$\frac{7}{8}$ DRILL

$3\frac{3}{8}$

$2\frac{3}{4}$

$7\frac{3}{8}$

Anna Jae

For this book, Clyde Runion carved a toy pistol and a racing car (facing page) out of yellow pine to show us the kinds of toys he used to make for his children.

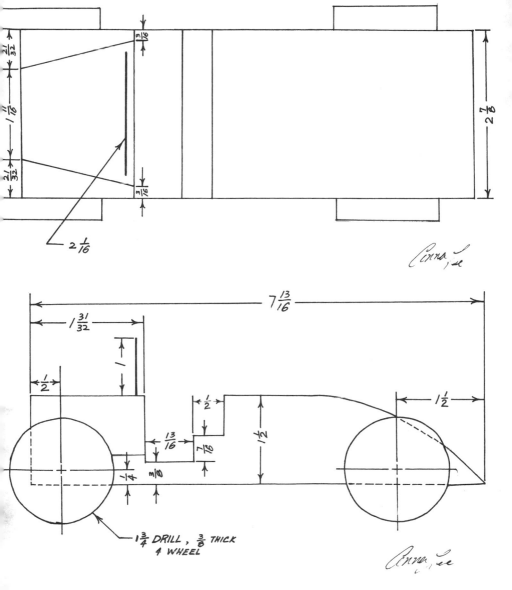

$\frac{21}{32}$

$\frac{3}{16}$

$1\frac{11}{16}$

$\frac{21}{32}$

$\frac{3}{16}$

$2\frac{7}{8}$

$2\frac{1}{16}$

Anna Lee

$7\frac{13}{16}$

$1\frac{31}{32}$

1

$\frac{1}{2}$

$\frac{1}{2}$

$1\frac{1}{2}$

$\frac{13}{16}$

$\frac{7}{16}$

$1\frac{1}{2}$

$\frac{1}{4}$

$\frac{3}{8}$

$1\frac{3}{4}$ DRILL , $\frac{3}{8}$ THICK
4 WHEEL

Anna Lee

two straight-back chairs. I had always loved interior decorating and things for the home. I kept this arranged on the dresser in the living room for it to be seen at all times. I received it from Santa when I was eight years old. I thought it was the prettiest gift I had ever gotten.

The next year I got a tiny china tea set. Boy, was I excited, for this was perfect. I set the tea set on the little table to look like a meal was about to be served. I treasured these items for many years.

After my two girls were born, they played with the things and slowly the items were broken or lost.

Edwina Rubel: [All my Christmases were pretty special], but I think one I remember most was when I got my tin kitchen. I thought I was going to get a doll and I didn't want a doll. My tin kitchen was my pride and joy! It was about three feet in total length and about two feet high, and the ends were like doors with hinges that opened and closed. It was just galvanized tin and it wasn't painted. It came with all kinds of cooking utensils, stock pots, fry pans, sauce pans, and it had little make-believe stove eyes. It didn't look like an electric stove because there were no electric stoves. It looked like a woodburning cookstove.

Oh, I played with it every day. I served all kinds of imaginary meals and made them up. I was the only one that used it. I didn't let anybody else use it, not even my sisters. I kept the little kitchen right where I knew where it was for years and years and years.

Clyde English: One year Santa put a pretty ribbon for my hair in my stocking. And I remember one time on

Christmas Eve when I was little I went to Clayton on a Saturday afternoon and I had a dollar to buy Christmas gifts. I bought a toothbrush for a dime for one of my brothers, and toothpaste and combs for the others. I made that dollar buy presents for my whole family. There were three other children and my mama and daddy.

"I made that dollar buy presents for my whole family."

Later on I remember making handkerchiefs to give. We would crochet lace to go around them or hemstitch them.

One year I wanted a necklace so bad. They called them lavaliers. I cut one out of a Sears and Roebuck catalog and wore it for days just to let them know what I wanted for Christmas. It was not a very subtle hint! I just wore it around my neck, cut out of paper. And got it! [Laugh.]

Ruthie Bradley: I got a little red wagon one Christmas when I was six years old. And a little monkey you would put up on a nail and it would go up and down a string. That was the best Christmas because it was something unusual. That wagon was the best thing in the world because we lived up on a hill, and you'd get in that wagon and ride down through there. Down the road. We'd have a time with that wagon.

And my grandfather one time made me a little horse out of cornstalks for Christmas. That was there in my stocking. I remember that little horse that he made for me.

A lucky child might receive a hand-carved covered wagon, driver, and mules like this one made by Willard Watson of Deep Gap, North Carolina.

Hubert Hooper: The very earliest and the most special Christmas I remember was when I was four years old, and I got my first tricycle. It was really an old-fashioned type of tricycle, very small; it just had a flat board with three wheels on it, one wheel in the front and two wheels in the back. I'd never seen anything like it before. I remember my first cousin came to the house, and together we rode it back and forth across the porch.

We sometimes made gifts, and I remember my mother making clothes. She'd make shirts or maybe pairs of pants for Christmas. Often she'd make underwear out of flour sacks. She'd get a twenty-five-pound sack of flour, empty the sack, and turn it inside out, and it would make really good material.

Louise Hooper: We had gifts under the Christmas tree, and they were wrapped, but we never had any boxes. We used rolls of crepe paper, and we wrapped everything in odd shapes.

My mother made dresses out of feed sacks as presents, and they were really pretty. They were entirely made out of cotton, and today they would really be popular. She would wash the sacks and cut them up, and she'd cut a pattern out of newspaper. Then she'd sew up each dress.

Lucille Ponder: I remember waking up one morning and finding a box of goodies under the bed. There was a big school tablet about two inches thick, rough paper, and it had a big 5 on the cover. And there were penny pencils that were made out of cedar. They were regular pencil length, and round, but they were slimmer. The erasers was glued in the end. No metal, just the cedar wood.

"I guess mostly what I remember is the smells that's linked with Christmas!"

I guess mostly what I remember is the smells that's linked with Christmas! For years, every time I smelled an orange, I thought of Christmas. That's when we got our oranges. And they were individually wrapped in what we called "the silk paper." The apples, too. Big apples. They were wrapped in paper.

Elmer Ponder: I remember the first present I ever got, other than socks. Now, we always got some socks. But the first present ever I got was a little stable made out of paper, with two or three little paper horses in it. They had harness on 'em. They was workhorses. And boy, to me that was the prettiest thing I ever seen in my life! And I played with it till I wore it out. The horses were little thin fellers, but they were made out of a stiff paper and they'd stand up on their little feet. And they had stalls in that little shed of a thing. And I could put 'em in there. That's the first present I ever remember getting [in the toy line].

We always had Christmas parties at school. Every room would have a little Christmas party and a tree and we'd have gifts under it. We'd draw names. Well, I'd already got three sets of dominoes the three years before. This year I never could find a box with my name on it. Well, the day we was gonna have the party, I got around and I kept huntin'. And way back over on the back side, in the corner, right down agin' the floor, there was a little box. And I noticed it had my name on it.

I eased the box out right gentle like and shook it and I heard dominoes rattling. That made the fourth set. That done me. I didn't need no more dominoes. I got four sets of dominoes in four years. Now, that ain't no tall tale. That's the truth.

We'd draw names early, way long before Christmas, and give everybody plenty of time to get presents. Hard up as people were and as little money as they was in the community, why they done pretty good. Wasn't too many children disappointed in their presents.

Nola Campbell: It was hard times back when I was a child, and when Christmas came, people enjoyed it. They really loved to see Christmas come. I'd get a new pair of

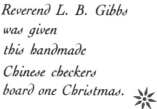

Reverend L. B. Gibbs
was given
this handmade
Chinese checkers
board one Christmas.

shoes every Christmas and I'd sleep with 'em on the first night. Since we didn't get but one pair a year, they had to do us. We could tear 'em up if we wanted to, but if we did we went barefooted. If we took care of 'em they lasted us all winter. When the first day of May came, I was tickled, because Mama'd let us go barefooted.

"I'd get a new pair of shoes every Christmas and I'd sleep with 'em on the first night."

Ruby Ivie: The girls got a little tea set. I used to get a set every Christmas until I got too old. Now the boys always got a new little Barlow knife, a cap pistol, or a harmonica. The girls would always blow on the harmonicas, but they hated those cap pistols.

Christine Wigington: Oh, it was a good time—all the slipping around, you know, trying to keep our gifts hid. As

long as any of us were at home, we got a gift for Christmas—
sometimes a pair of beads or a handkerchief or a pair of
stockings or something else that we could use. [It wouldn't
ever be anything that cost very much money because] we
had a hard time [financially] on a farm back then. We only
got ten cents a pound for cotton. We didn't have much but
we had a good time. I lived through three severe depres-
sions. Back then, though, we didn't know it. We always
had enough to eat.

Addie Norton: [Lots has changed.] My boys didn't
have any toys or games, only something that they made.
The last two had more than the first two because the older
boys would get them things. They'd make them a wheel
and get a little stick and put a piece across there and roll
that thing in front of them. They'd get up there on the hill
and come down there just a-flying.

People this day and time, if they've got any children,
they don't have but one or two anymore. People used to
have seven or eight, you know, and up to twelve or thirteen. And they couldn't give them much. But this day and
time people gives their children so much that they don't
pay no attention to any of it. They kick a toy around—it's
all over the house; it's kicked out in the yard; it's played
with no time at all.

Louise and Hubert Hooper: My mother was left an
orphan when she was ten years old, and she had two
younger sisters. She had to quit school so she'd have time
to raise those children. For her, I guess, Christmas was just
another day, besides hearing about Jesus at church.

Because they had grown up in such hard times, our

parents didn't really make a big thing of Christmas. We didn't have much when it came to gifts. What we really looked forward to was the fun we had at church and school and the good food. We always had to have plenty of food on the table, because we didn't have anything else. It also meant a lot to us to give presents to my younger brother—he was six years younger than my sister and I. When we got older, we always wanted him to have more toys. We wanted to play Santa Claus with him.

The spiritual element of Christmas was much more important to people then than it is now, or even than it was when our kids were grown up. By the time our kids were growing up, it had already become pretty materialistic.

"Things don't mean that much in life. It's what you do for other people and how you treat other people. When you leave this earth, you can't take a house with you, or pretty clothes, or cars, or nothing. It's all left."

Things don't mean that much in life. It's what you do for other people and how you treat other people. When you leave this earth, you can't take a house with you, or pretty clothes, or cars, or nothing. It's all left. We all go just like we came.

DOLLS

Aunt Mo Norton: My mother made the rag doll that I got. She'd made the dolls six, eight, and ten inches long. It didn't take her too long to make the dolls—about a couple of hours. She'd made them out of old rags. She stuffed them with cotton, or some people stuffed them with old rags because cotton cost money. She used buttons for the eyes, buttons for the nose, and she just drawed the mouth on there. Sometimes she would work the mouth on with a needle, like embroidery, and she made the clothes out of any kind of material she had.

Annie Perry: We didn't have no cornhusk dolls. We didn't know how to make those things. Had rag dolls. Dolls made out of rags. Roll up a rag and tie a string around its neck and we had a doll.

Louise Coldren: We had homemade dolls, rag dolls. [We took] cloth and cut out a shape of a doll, put corn shucks in it, cotton, or old stockings, and painted a face on the dolls. You could make hair out of yarn.

Bertha Dockins: We used to have these old black stockings and we made rag dolls from them. We'd take a needle and some white thread, and make their eyes and nose and mouth. We stuffed them with bran or something like that.

Janet Van Winkle: The story behind the doll pattern is it started with my great-great-grandma, I think. Best I can remember, this was my great-great-grandpa's idea.

MATERIALS NEEDED:

small stocking with fold-down cuff (man's sock may be used for large doll)

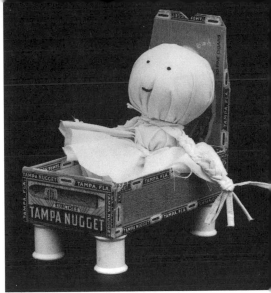

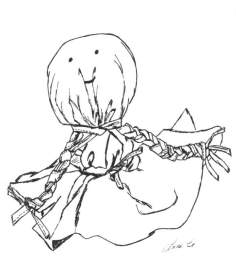

*A simple, homemade rag doll
in a cigar box bed satisfied
many girls at Christmas.*

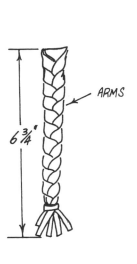

ARMS

6¾"

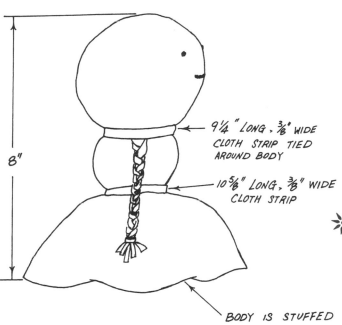

8"

9¼" LONG, ⅜" WIDE
CLOTH STRIP TIED
AROUND BODY

10⅝" LONG, ⅜" WIDE
CLOTH STRIP

BODY IS STUFFED
WITH COTTON

batting

buttons and other trim

yarn or cord

red and black embroidery floss

Cut off toe area one or two inches, according to size of sock. Split in half for ends of toes to form legs. Stuff the legs of doll and heel of sock with batting. Stuff heel of sock very full so doll will sit; continue stuffing to cuff, and tie with yarn or cord. Turn down cuff to form cap. Tie with yarn or cord to form head.

Stitch ends and sides of each cut toe piece; stuff and attach to the body. Make arms reach forward or up. Add features (small buttons for eyes, embroider mouth or nose).

Icie Rickman: We also made dolls and gave them to each other for Christmas. We made little rag dolls, shuck dolls, and cob dolls. To make a shuck doll, first you just take the shucks and stand it down. You put rubber bands around the shucks to keep the doll's shape. Next you just wad up some cloth and make its head. The hands and arms of the doll are simply one shuck laid horizontally across its stomach which sticks out of both sides. Then I make its little skirt.

To make a corn cob doll, you just kindly take it and scrape out a little place for its eyes with a knife. Then you mark the eyes, nose, and mouth with a pencil, or something black. You dress it kind of like the shuck dolls.

Gail McClure: Grandma [Sallie Hale] said that she never got a doll for Christmas. The only doll she ever had was made of an ear of corn. Her mother made its head, arms, and body out of stuffed cloth and attached it to the corn cob.

Harriet Echols: Father wouldn't buy dolls. Back then people had to work for a living, and Dad didn't believe in

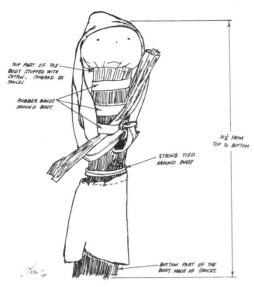

Icie Rickman with an armload of homemade rag dolls. Also pictured is a shuck doll she made.

foolishness, and so we didn't have any toys. My older sister made my first doll, and I guess I was eight or ten years old. We made rag dolls and cornshuck dolls, and then we learned to do potato heads where you take potatoes and make a doll. You get one big potato and get sticks and make its legs. Then you get a smaller potato and make its head, and find sticks for its arms. A potato will last a long time.

"... Dad didn't believe in foolishness, and so we didn't have any toys."

Edith Darnell: A doll was real special because we never saw a store-bought doll that much back up in here. The young'uns didn't have dolls, unless we made them ourselves. We'd take sticks and make them. We used a little stick for her arms and legs. Then we would dress them up.

Ruby Ivie: The girls would usually get a little doll. Sometimes the dolls would have china heads and stuffed bodies, arms, and legs. They might even have little china hands and shoes.

The largest doll I ever had was a pretty sleepy-doll. It closed its eyes when you laid it on its back. It was prettier than any doll I ever had, and more like the dolls are now. I wanted to save it because it was the prettiest and largest one I ever received. I had one little sister five years younger than I, and she liked my doll better than she did her own doll. I hated not to let her play with it, so I would get it out of my mama's trunk and let her play with it. Eventually she pulled its hair out and tore its clothes off. Mama kept telling me not to let her tear that doll up. I think she played with the doll until she got tired of it. That was my first doll I really cherished.

Lucy Hyatt: We'd get little store-bought dolls. I remember getting the prettiest one. It was a little china doll. She had on a little gold necklace; it was painted on. That was the most special present I ever got. I was old enough to know who Santa Claus was by then.

Ethel Corn: Mama used to make dolls, and then you could also get rag dolls in the stores. Then they went to making dolls with just their heads filled, and then sleepy dolls. I was a pretty good-sized young'un before I ever saw any sleepy dolls.

I can remember my first doll. They had just come out with what they called the Dutch doll. Their body would be stuffed with straw, but their arms and legs and faces would be delft. My sister and I had sleepy dolls, and mine wouldn't go to sleep. My brother, Mel, was always doing something, and he told me to take my doll and hit it over the plow handle and it would go to sleep. I did, and it broke that doll's head all to pieces. It was made out of the same thing that cups and saucers were made of.

"We'd cut doll clothes like we'd cut dresses for a baby, and after I got older, that was the way I learned to cut and sew."

We'd cut doll clothes like we'd cut dresses for a baby, and after I got older, that was the way I learned to cut and sew.

Gertrude Keener: For Christmas I got one doll. It was the gift I enjoyed most. I was about five years old, I guess, and the little doll didn't have any clothes on, so the fun was making clothes for the doll. It had little glass feet and glass eyes, and it had a bonnet on its head. My mother gave it to me.

We also cut out little paper dollies. We gave them just like they were. Just cut them out of paper.

Clyde English: Here's an old doll that I've kept all these years. Part of it is made of china. It was in this box, and this poor thing is so old that its hair is falling out. But it was in this box, and it says on the outside that it costs twenty-five cents. Another doll like this, no telling what it would bring as an antique now.

The best one I ever got was a little doll, and its face was made out of the material that if it gets damp or gets old, it would come off. I named it Gordon. I remember a few years ago, I threw it away. My mother said, "You threw Gordon away!" I loved that doll so much, but it had lost all the skin off its face and just left that old raw-looking material that it was made out of.

Mrs. E. H. Brown: There's the only toy I ever owned in my life. [She shows us a little, old doll.] I wouldn't take a nickel for that thing. The dress is old, but not as old as the head. I've played with that thing, you know, and I've worn out several dresses and had to have more dresses made. I expect it would be at least seventy years old, maybe seventy-five.

You had to make [the body], and fit it to that little

Clyde English has saved these two china dolls she received as Christmas gifts.

head. That's all there was. Now that's Pard—that's her name. That was my partner, you know, and I called her Pard.

SANTA CLAUS

Giving up the myth of Santa is one of the events in a child's life when he or she begins to cross the line into adulthood. The revelation is sometimes funny, like the case of Irene Galyou, who found out that Santa was her dad because she recognized the shoes he had on; sometimes it is traumatic, like the time Janie P. Taylor found out Santa was being played by her dad at a school Christmas get-together. There are people, like Burma Patterson, who found out there wasn't a Santa Claus but still believe in him anyway.

This chapter, then, is largely about how people discovered that Santa Claus is a real person and not a person who lives at the North Pole surrounded by reindeer and elves.

—Robbie Bailey

Ada Crone: I remember one night, I lived with my grandmother, but I went to stay awhile with my daddy and mother. It was Christmas and I wanted to see Santa Claus. I'd heard a lot about him, never had seen him. But I thought I'd play a trick on my mother and daddy that night and see Santa Claus.

We lived in a log house and it had a rock chimney to it. Well, they'd always tell me that Santa Claus come down the chimney. We'd hang our stockings up by the fireplace. They made us go to bed early that night. I was pretty small, but I can remember it. I told my mother I wanted my head up a little bit higher—it wasn't high enough. I had one pillow, and she got another one and put under my head, and still it wasn't high enough. I told her it wasn't high enough; I wanted another one. She got some coats and put it under my head. And I was sittin' up in the bed by that time. My mama said, "What do you want your head so high for?"

I said, "Oh, I just want it that way. I can't sleep with my head down low." Well, I finally had my head high enough. I thought I could turn around and see Santy when he came down the chimney. But by that time I was so sleepy I couldn't stay awake, and I went to sleep and I never did get to see Santa Claus.

Doris Shumate: It was during the Depression. We didn't have much. [My boy] was about as big as you are, six or seven years old. He had this little picture of a wagon. You'd find it in his britches pocket. There was seven of us. Somehow, we got enough together, borrowed it or something, to get him this wagon. Double wheels behind it, and little sideboards on it, you know. Christmas morning we had it settin' down at the foot of his bed. He dearly believed in Santy Claus. I mean to tell you. We had it settin' down at the foot of his bed, and Herman got up to build a fire. And he waked him up, and he just raised up and looked down to see that wagon, and he said, "God bless old Santy's heart." And just fell back in the bed.

Annie Thurmond: We had a fireplace, and we used to say Santa Claus came down the chimney. [Some of the older children got curious about Santa Claus] so they put ashes around the hearth to see if they could get Santa Claus's footprints! Well, the next morning, there'd be a footprint there. I can remember my daddy would get up on Christmas morning as early as we'd get up, or before, and get a big fire in the fireplace so we'd be warm. Then he'd sit there and enjoy [the children seeing that footprint and everyone opening their stockings] as much as we did.

"My grandmother remembers her dad being more excited on Christmas morning than the children were."

Nicole Skeen: My grandmother [Lula Skeen] remembers her dad being more excited on Christmas morning than the children were. He was always up by four building fires and dragging the children out of bed to see what Santa had brought them. She says that he believed in Santa more than the children did.

David North: Christmas morning in respect to chores was no different from any other. [My friend, Hal Hodgson,] would get up even earlier so he could eat an early breakfast with the family. They would have smoked sausage, eggs that he had gathered, milk, and biscuits with white gravy.

After breakfast, the entire family gathered around to wait on Santa Claus to walk through the door. "I know when I was young I did not even realize it was Daddy dressed up," says Hal. Hal is now seventy-five years old, but he still smiles when he tells this story.

Lela Maud Dean: As small children, there were seven of us. We thought if we were very good, Santa would come. I remember one Christmas, I wanted so hard to help my mother. We had to carry water from the spring. As I trotted along helping Mama, I just knew Santa would know how good I had been.

My aunt told us if we really listened, we could hear his sleigh bells long before Santa knocked at the door.

Shortly after dark, we grew very quiet, and sure enough, very faintly, we heard the jingle of bells. When my dad opened the door, sure enough, there was Santa, my uncle, with a pack and all.

Mattie Pearl McGaha: I especially remember when I was a child about three or four years old. Santa Claus was at Snow Hill Baptist Church and he gave me a little swing. When he called my name and started toward me, I got down under the seat. I didn't stop until I was way back under several people's seats before somebody caught me. I was afraid of him.

Hazel Duvall McWherter: We always spent Christmas with my grandfather and grandmother. I guess I was fifteen years old before we ever spent a Christmas at home. And at this particular time, my father and mother owned a grocery store, and we were going to my grandfather's to spend Christmas. My aunt and uncle and their one child and my sister and I were going, and we didn't get to go until after the store closed. They only had dirt tracks [for roads] in those days, and we went in the track. We got snowbound. It had snowed all day, and there was about fourteen inches of snow. We got halfway, and the track was snowbound. We couldn't go any farther. So my father and my uncle got out of the truck and went to my grandfather's to get a team of mules.

This was about eight o'clock at night, and I can remember my sister and my cousin and I, we cried until they got back because we were afraid Santa Claus was coming before we got there and he wouldn't know where to bring our gifts. I was probably six years old.

It was around midnight when they got back with the team of mules, and they pulled us into our grandfather's. He was sitting there waiting for us. We started crying because we just knew Santa Claus had come down the chimney before we got there. To prove to us that he hadn't been there, he took two cookies and put them on a napkin, and set down a glass of milk on the hearth.

I was wondering how Santa Claus was going to come down that chimney with a fire in there and not get his whiskers burnt. But anyway, when I got up the next morning, he showed me that glass, the milk was gone and the cookies had been eaten. And we knew that Santa had been there.

Janie P. Taylor: I was in the first grade in what is now South Rabun [Elementary School]. The Christmas program at the Tiger School, as it was called at that time, was a big deal. Grades one through seven all were brought into the auditorium. In there was this massive Christmas tree decorated with the tinsel; it didn't have as many elaborate balls and lights as we have now, but nevertheless it was majestic. Everybody was so excited! We marched first, being the first graders.

After everyone had performed, then came time for Santa Claus to appear. Now I had heard rumors about how Santa Claus was really Mama and Daddy, but I had never quite believed this before. But then Santa came out on the stage, and he was my daddy! He had donated his time to come to the school and play Santa Claus. I started crying, and the teachers had to take me back to the classroom. My father was so upset. After the program, nothing would do but for me to go home with my daddy. As I walked beside him, and as he carried the despised Santa Claus outfit, we talked, and I will always remember Daddy saying, "Life is full of surprises—especially at Christmastime."

Marinda Brown: At the place where we lived then, the house was on one side of a pretty good-sized stream, and our springhouse where the milk and butter were kept was on the other side. When I was about five or six, maybe not that old, my oldest brother got in the springhouse and he would go "Ho, ho, ho!" in a big loud voice, playing Santa Claus, you know. We had a foot log to cross the creek to get from the house to the springhouse. One brother and one sister got me in between them and got me across that foot log and got me up to the springhouse, and this other brother stuck candy out the cracks of the spring-house and would go "Ho, ho, ho!" I was terrified. I wouldn't go get that candy; I was scared to death!

We had a bunch of cousins that came to visit us along just before Christmas one time. They were older than we were. I must have been about ten. They told us that our mother and dad were playing Santa Claus, and we wouldn't believe it. They said, "Well, we'll just show you!" And they found out where our Christmas things that were going in our stockings were hid, and they showed them to us. That happened just before Christmas, and I was terribly disappointed. See, we children back then didn't learn things like you children do now. You know everything that's going on, and back then, we didn't.

Iris Patterson: On rainy days or Sundays after church, our dad would make me toys. He made the boys guns that he whittled from wood. He made the girls spoons and forks from wood, and dishes from acorns. I have made some of the same designs of cups and saucers from acorns.

But I was fourteen or fifteen years old when I learned how the store-bought gifts were gotten. I had heard rumors that Santa was your parents, but I refused to believe it, for we saw no gifts or knew of none until we awoke on Christmas morning. However, I was rather sad when I did know for sure because it was so much fun believing. I learned when my dad come home from work one Saturday and called me aside. He gave me some money and said for me to go buy Christmas presents for the younger children. I decided to be real careful with the money so as to make it buy as much as possible. I was so proud when I began to choose gifts to have enough money to get every one of us a gift, even Daddy. I got my older sister and myself a comb and mirror set. The four boys got cap pistols. My younger sister got a doll, and I found a white handkerchief for Daddy. [And that's how I learned there was no Santa.]

Hazel Duvall McWherter: I remember the first time I learned there wasn't a Santa Claus. It's never been Christmas since. I slept upstairs, and there was a little hole in the floorboards upstairs, and I could see down. My daddy woke me up trying to put things in my stocking. I saw Papa putting a little plastic bathtub and a little doll in my stocking, and Christmas has never been the same.

Billy Long: Santa Claus was about the same as he is today, but he didn't have red clothes like he's got today. We thought he came down the chimney usually. Every Christmas we kept listening for him but we never seen him

80

but one time. That time he brought us some candy and came in the front door. I was about six years old. He asked me what I wanted for Christmas. Then he jumped up directly and said, "Oh, Lord! Them deers are leaving me. I got to go." He went to hollering, "Ho, ho," and went out the door after 'em. I knew who it was, but I played ignorant, you know. To him, I didn't know who it was.

Ruby Ivie: Before Christmas our parents would talk about the excitement of the holiday coming. They were not too strict about the traditions of Santa Claus. They allowed us to believe there was a secret man named Santa Claus who would bring us presents after midnight. That's what my parents said.

[After I married], my husband cut off part of his finger one time right before Christmas, and our children asked him what they were going to get. Well, he shook his head and said, "Well, I don't guess you'll have Christmas this year." They asked him, "Why not?" and he said, "Because Santa got his finger cut off!" They gave him the funniest looks and got a kick out of it.

Deirdre Stubblefield: On Christmas Eve, everyone would gather in the bedroom, sit down on the beds, and wait for Santa to come. My grandmother [Ida Neal] recalled one exceptional Christmas when Santa leaned over to pick up a gift and his beard got too close to one of the candles, and it caught on fire. Of course the beard was fake, but Santa would not pull it off in front of the children. He ran out of the room before he pulled it off.

Gertrude Keener: I heard my mother tearing strips of paper, and I wasn't asleep 'cause I was thinking about Santa Claus. I'd always wondered about Santa Claus, and I heard my mother tearing strips of paper, and I peeped at the foot of my bed to see what she was doing. I was about five years old, I guess. Then I went back to bed. And after that, I helped my mother fix the stockings for the younger children.

Burice Bradshaw: We was told about Santa by a girlfriend, and I still have a hard feeling toward her because we truly believed in Santa Claus. We told her we didn't believe her. She said, "Well, you just go home and look and see if you don't get it." So we did. Mama had our dolls hid in a trunk. It broke my heart. It was the biggest letdown in my life when I found out about it.

Leona Carver: I was about seven or eight, I guess, before I thought there wasn't no Santa Claus, because back then we never did even see oranges or apples and candy. After a while I guess I just had an idea because the best livers then that could afford them would get real nice things, you know, and us poor people never did get much. [Laughter.] We called them the best livers.

I did get a doll off of the Christmas tree at church, and they said Santa Claus brought it to me. It was the most special gift I got [because] it was the first doll I had got. It was a bought doll. When I growed up, I found out Miss Helen Grist at church was the one that bought it.

Claude Hollifield: All the excitement on Christmas Eve day was anticipating what you were going to get from

Santa Claus. I got a pocketknife and some firecrackers and a little cap pistol. I ain't even seen any of them in years! I got a French harp one time—G-key, whatever that means. Blew that thing, but never did learn to play a tune on it, so I never did get no more of them.

Marie Hollifield: We always put a drink and something to eat on the table for Santa Claus the night he was to come. It would disappear, so we thought he came. I remember us looking out the back door and tracking him one time. We almost always got snow on Christmas back then, seems to me, and I guess Daddy went out and made those tracks in the back door through the snow.

My favorite gift was a doll, and I once got a bicycle. The reason Claude didn't get another French harp was that he made too much racket with it!

Jill Martin: Grandma [Pauline Wilson] found out about Santa when she saw a receipt from Sears where a gift came from.

Gail Hepburn: The funniest Christmas Irene Galyou remembers is that time her uncle dressed up in a Santa Claus suit. Irene and her sister recognized him by his shoes.

Burma Patterson: We were brought up to believe in Santa Claus, and there's still a Santa Claus for me. There always will be. The longest day I live, there'll be a Santa Claus. I think the spirit of Christmas is Santa Claus—is giving.

FOUR
Food and Menus

Edited by Amy Nichols

❋ Father had gone out early that Christmas Eve morning and killed the turkey that he had been fattening up for several months. Then he replenished the stack of wood on the porch that Mother had been using up almost as fast as Father could bring more. She had been working hard all week preparing the special food for Christmas dinner. When Mother made the gingerbread men to go on the tree, she would let me cut them out. During that week before Christmas, we could have all the apples out of the cellar that we wanted. Sometimes we would eat so many apples that we would get sick. Mother always warned us, but we didn't pay any attention to her. When she had all of the breads and cakes cooked, she would put a clean white cloth over them to keep them fresh. She put the pies in the pie safe.

I'll always remember those Christmas dinners; they were so special. It seems that Christmas was always memorable because we sat at our small table and thanked God for being able to spend another Christmas together.

Sometimes in the earlier years, Christmas was celebrated by a week-long celebration of neighbors visiting their friends or relatives. Sorghum candy was made for candy pullings. Sometimes cakes were made for each day of the week before Christmas. Food has always played a large part in the celebration of Christmas.

In this chapter, there are two main sections. The first consists of specific memories of Christmas dinners, desserts, and other treats. The second part is recipes, some of which are as unique as cornbread dressing, Grandmother's traditional pie, and apple stack cake.

The recipes from long ago haven't changed drastically from the ones of today, but it's much easier today to prepare the Christmas dinner than it was then. Today we run to the grocery store, pick up a frozen turkey and packaged dressing, and buy a dessert at the bakery. Everything you need is at the local grocery store. There is no time spent raising a turkey or canning vegetables. It seems so much easier.

In many ways Christmas dinners are as good today as they once were. But there is something about having home-grown food cooked on a wood stove that is still appealing.

—Amy Nichols

"I've seen her make dinner out of what anyone else would think was nothing at all—and make a good dinner!"
Lyndall "Granny" Toothman

Lyndall "Granny" Toothman is seventy-eight years old but has the heart and energy of a teenager and looks like a perfect granny.

She has an apartment in Kentucky, but she doesn't stay there much of the time, because she travels around the country in a small van in which she lives and cooks. She teaches weaving and spinning at craft festivals that take her all over the country. This may sound unusual, but the most unusual thing is that she spins and weaves using dog, cat, and rabbit hair as well as sheep's wool.

One spring she stayed with us at Foxfire for a week. She came into the classroom and told us stories of her childhood Christmases.

> —Clark Bowen, Kim Baldwin, Kevin Cannon, and Richard Harmon

Lyndall "Granny" Toothman: When I was very small, we lived in a little log house back in the mountains of West Virginia. My sister was six years older than I was, and while I was growing up, it was just her and me until I was fifteen years old. Then, when my mother was forty-five, my brother was born. But until then, I was the boy of the family. I wore blue jeans from the time I can remember. Dad took me everywhere with him. I didn't do anything in the house. My sister did the housework, and I drove the

86

horses and milked the cows and done everything that a boy would do. Dad would take me out in the hay field, and he and I would get the hay up and in better shape than our neighbor who had two boys, both of them older than I was.

I was awful handy. I even learned to juggle. I finally got to where I could keep three balls in the air. Being a lone child that way, I learned to entertain myself. I'd thump a ball against the barn for hours at a time—thump, thump, thump, thump—until Mother'd get so sick of it, she'd yell, "Stop that!"

And I had a hoop with a little stick. I rolled that miles and miles and miles. Everywhere I'd go, I'd take my stick and my hoop and down the road I'd run. I never walked. I don't remember walking until I was in high school! I'd take that hoop and go down the road, or I'd have a ball pitching it up and catching it as I went. I was *always* doing something with my hands wherever I went and whatever I'd do, and that's the reason you see me using my hands a lot today. I still use my hands all the time.

Now whenever Christmas came around, some of the neighbors decorated their homes, but we didn't until I was nearly grown. Then I went out and got a tree; but in my early childhood, I don't remember decorating at all.

We always decorated the church, though. We just had a *big* Christmas tree there—usually a hemlock or a spruce—and everybody got together and we strung miles and miles of popcorn. If the weather was good, we would pick little red mountain tea berries and string them. And then we made the paper trimmings, these little colored paper chains. My mother was quite handy with paper, and she made beautiful roses—you almost thought they were real. And they'd put mountain laurel and rhododendron around in the church.

Then they'd have a Christmas program, and that was always a big thing. I remember that we was always in the Christmas program. I would usually have a little poem to say or something like that. And they always had the nativity scene and the shepherds and the angels and the cradle and the Baby, and once in a while we'd have a live animal or two and bring in like a little donkey or a lamb.

We'd have the whole community gathered in, and we had Santa Claus, and everybody got a little gift. Even if it was just a piece of stick candy, everybody got a little gift. And if somebody wanted to give you something else, then they'd put your name on it and put it under the Christmas tree.

That reminds me of a little story you might be interested in. Our land lay something like this here in northern Georgia. Back in the mountains we had a wagon road from the little town of Williamsburg over to Richwood which was ten or twelve miles away. Off of that road, right on top of Cole Knob, there's a path went out, and six miles out that path, during Prohibition times, a man came in there and he was making moonshine. There was nine miles of old fields on top of the mountain—beautiful land, plenty of cold springs—so he grew his corn and was making moonshine.

Then he brought a fifteen-year-old girl in as his wife, and he kept her back in there, and over about ten years, four sons was born. One day in the fall of the year when her husband was gone, the lady of the family decided she'd had it. She marched out of there with a little pack on her back and left those four kids. The youngest one was about six and the oldest was ten.

Lyndall
"Granny"
Toothman.

Well, when he came back and seen that she was gone, he gathered his stuff and left, too. Left them four kids back there by themselves. Very few people went back in there, but later on a few of his old drinking buddies went back to his moonshine still and found the kids back in there still living in that tarpaper shack. They weren't starved to death — they had some chickens and so they'd had a few eggs, and they had some potatoes, and the oldest boy could milk the cow — but they were pretty well distressed. Their clothes weren't much good anyhow, and they were getting ragged and it was about wintertime. Fact is, it was almost Christmas.

". . . later on a few of his old drinking buddies went back to his moonshine still and found the kids back in there still living in that tarpaper shack."

89

So they brought them four boys out. They had never went to school, and they had seen very few people before. And this Christmas the community knew about those boys and they made a special Christmas. It was the first Christmas that these boys had ever known anything about. All of us chipped in and got them some clothes and different things. They had never tasted an orange or a banana or candy or anything like that, and they'd never seen Santa Claus—it was all way beyond those boys' imaginations. And they just couldn't imagine all those people. There must have been seventy-five or maybe a hundred in the church for this special program; and during the program when they was bringing in the live donkey into the manger they had set up in there, the ten-year-old boy jumped up in the church and yelled, "My God, I didn't know that there was this many people in the whole world!"

But the boys enjoyed it all. The little one got scared and cried when Santa Claus came out. That scared him because he didn't know there was such a thing as Christmas.

When spring came, the oldest boy run off and disappeared, but the three other boys stayed, and the next fall they got them in school and they stayed there in the community for years.

"My daddy always gave me a dollar on Christmas. That was a lot of money . . . I could make it last six months."

My daddy always gave me a dollar on Christmas. We'd put up our stockings the night before, and the next morning it would be in there along with some stick candy and an orange. That was a lot of money. And there was no

restrictions on that dollar. I could give it to somebody if I
wanted to, or spend it however I wanted to. My sister liked
pretty things, so she always bought pretty things for herself with her dollar; but with my dollar, I'd keep it and buy
candy and chewing gum and give treats to the kids. I'd still
have some of that dollar left way up until the end of school.
I could take a penny and get as much candy as you could
with fifty cents today, so I could make it last six months.

One Christmas—I must have been eleven or twelve, a
little bit between growing up and still being a little child—my
parents asked me, "Now would you like for us to have a
Christmas and kinda play Santa Claus this year, or would
you druther have your dollar?" Well, I decided that I
wanted them to go and give me a surprise for Christmas
morning.

We had a dresser that had one locked drawer. It was
in the middle of the dresser. There was an unlocked drawer
ahead of it and one below it. They put all these gifts in this
dresser drawer and locked it up and hid the key. Well, I
got a little too curious, so before Christmas I took out the
top drawer and there was the middle drawer with all the
things in it—a doll, and a little teddy bear they'd got me,
and a pocket knife. That was the first year I'd got a good
pocket knife. And a few other little odds and ends that you
could get for a dollar or a little better. I expect they spent a
little bit more on that Christmas than they usually did. But
I spoiled it all.

They knew I'd gotten into the drawer. Things was
kinda misplaced in there! [Laughter.] The next Christmas,
I went back to the dollar.

We didn't have too much to go on, but we always had
plenty to eat. My mother was an excellent cook, and I've

seen her make dinner out of what anyone else would think was nothing at all—and make a good dinner. Now on Christmas Day, we didn't have the traditional Christmas dinner that the neighbors did. We had a special dinner that all of us looked forward to all year. And sometimes we would have to begin preparing for it three months before. The dinner consisted of fried country ham—we always cured our own meat—and red-eye gravy. I guess you all know what country ham and red-eye gravy is. Then we had baked Irish potatoes and baked sweet potatoes, a pot of leather breeches beans, potato salad, dandelion salad, deviled eggs—we always had deviled eggs—hot raised biscuits, corn pone, jellies, jams, and preserves, three or four different kinds of homemade pickles, and we always had plenty of milk and butter. We also had either strawberry or dandelion wine. Then for dessert it was always boiled custard and Lady Baltimore white cake, and for the children they also had chestnuts.

Now do you want me to tell you how to fix some of those things? Some of them were fairly unusual dishes which even our neighbors didn't usually do, but we thought they were great things.

"I guess the most unusual item was the dandelion salad."

I guess the most unusual item was the dandelion salad. In the fall, about October when things died down, we would get dandelion roots and put them in a box that had a little soil in the bottom so the roots could adhere. Then we'd go out in the woods and pull the leaves aside and get that soft rich wood pummy soil and put about eight to ten inches of that over the top of those roots, and put that box down in the cellar in a dark place. About a month before Christmas, we'd bring that box out and put it in a nice warm sunny window and begin watering those roots, and they'd shoot up through that pummy soil. The reason for having it so deep is that you want the dandelion leaves to be as long as you can get them. They come up yellow until they get out of the soil to the light, and then they turn green, but what you want mostly is those yellow leaves, and the longer they are, the more tender they are. We liked them in six- to eight-inch yellow spikes with little tips of green on the top.

To prepare them for the meal, we would wash those leaves and chop them in bite sizes and put them in our bowl, and then we took a half cup of apple cider vinegar, a half cup of water, a good tablespoon of sugar, a teaspoon-ful of salt, and we'd mix that all thoroughly so that the salt and the sugar was all melted. Then we got about three spoonfuls of good ham grease from where we'd fried out our ham, and we took this liquid and poured it all in our hot skillet. While it was still hot, we poured it over the dandelions. If we had some green onions, we especially liked to put a few of them in there. And that made a salad that we thought was great!

If we didn't pull the whole plant up to get the leaves, we'd let the roots stay in that box and keep sprouting them and we'd have several messes after Christmas. They'll come up in a second and a third time.

Another fairly unusual thing we had was the corn pone. Now I know you've all heard of corn pone, but I don't know whether any of you has eaten the *real* corn pone or not. It is something like salt-rising bread. You take two cups of stone ground cornmeal, one cup of all-purpose flour (don't use the "hopped up" kind), two tablespoonfuls of sugar, one tablespoonful of salt, and three cups of boiling hot water, and you want your water really boiling hot! You stir that down into your cornmeal until it gets real smooth. If you get your water good and hot, it's rather thick, and you stir that around until you get all the lumps out of it. Be careful and pour your hot water in slowly; kinda make a hole in the middle of the flour and begin stirring around and stir your water in there, and then you put that in a warm place. It should be up around ninety degrees. We'd always fix our wood stove so it would stay warm all night, and we'd set that maybe on the back of the stove or in the warming closet. Or you could put it up against the warm rocks of the fireplace. You might turn it a time or two during the night so that all the sides'd be even and it'd be fine in the morning. But you don't want to put a tight lid on it. You want to put a porous dish towel on the top of it so it can collect the air yeast. You know all old cabins where you make a lot of bread mean you've got a lot of yeast in the air, and you want to catch that natural yeast. Overnight the dough kinda ferments. The worse it smells in the morning, the better it's going to be! If it smells real bad, you know it's begun to ferment and it's going to be good. It takes about twelve to eighteen hours. When the bubbles begin to raise and it gets kinda spongy, it's ready. It's something like the old sourdough biscuit bread. You can tell by the smell of it when it's done.

Then you take a mixture of one level teaspoon of baking soda, two tablespoons of melted shortening (I prefer meat fryings myself), and two tablespoons of sorghum syrup, and you stir that in there. You want the dough kinda sloppy-like. If you think it's gotten too thick, put just a little buttermilk in it. Sweet milk will do, but buttermilk's better because it raises the soda better. Put maybe a fourth of a cup or something like that and stir it in there, but remember that is not really necessary. After you get all that stirred in there, you put it *directly* in your oven. We always had a Dutch oven already greased and hot with a little cornmeal sprinkled in it so the pone'll put out from the pan good. Let that meal get just a little browned on the bottom and around the sides, put in the dough, and then put the oven back in the fireplace where the air won't strike it too much. Set it on hot coals and ashes, and pile coals on the lid, and about every hour and a half, reach in and get some fresh coals raked underneath it and piled on the top. It takes most of the day to cook it, but you want to cook it until it browns all the way around and the sides begin to pull out away from the oven. It doesn't taste like any other bread that you've ever eaten. You don't taste the cornmeal. You don't taste any one thing. It's just an all-over—well, it's great! We always wanted some of it hot right then with butter on it as soon as it was done, but you start eating it and you don't want anything else, usually! And the next day, as long as it lasts, you can slice it and fry it in butter like you do mush because it's a little sticky and soft, a little bit like spoon bread.

Since I don't have the fireplace now to cook on, sometimes I make one out of doors at the barbecue pit. And sometimes I put the Dutch oven down in one of these seven-quart enamel canners and put about four inches of water in that and set the oven on the rack inside and put the lid on and steam it gently for about five hours in that water. Then I take it out and put it in the electric oven and leave it at a temperature of about 325 degrees until it browns all over. It's just not as good cooked in an electric stove, though. It dries out and it just is not as good. When I cook it that way, I always double the recipe that I gave you and I fill that Dutch oven up to within an inch and a half of the top. I like to have it *full* so it'll raise up. Lots of times when I lift the lid off, it's stuck to the lid!

For that Christmas dinner we also had the hot raised biscuits—they weren't yeast rolls, but they was a combination of yeast and the traditional buttermilk and soda. We'd let them raise for about fifteen minutes and they'd get nice and fluffy, and we'd stick those in the oven of the wood cookstove.

We'd put both the Irish and the sweet potatoes down in the fireplace in the ashes, and we'd leave them in there about two hours, and by Christmas dinner, they'd be good and mushy done. Mother always saved our sweet potatoes up in the attic in a box full of sand. And the dried leather breeches beans had soaked all night in water, and the next day they'd get cooked on the wood stove in fresh water with a piece of bacon or ham hock for about three or four hours until they was good and tender. They have a taste all their own. Dad especially liked them.

The desserts weren't all that unusual. They still have recipes in the old books for the Lady Baltimore white cake. It was just a moist butter cake in layers. I remember it took almost a pound of butter—real butter, too, and not this imitation that we have now, but the real stuff that you churned up and down in the churn. And eight egg whites. That left eight yolks to put in our boiled custard, so it was a good combination of desserts and nothing was wasted there. Once in a while we might put real raspberry jelly or something like that between the cake's layers and then put coconut icing on it. We would trade eggs at the store for that coconut. It was always shredded in a package.

The custard was made out of just plain sugar, eggs, flour to thicken it, and whole milk, cream and all. You had to be very careful with it. We didn't have a double boiler then, so we'd take one pan and put it in a little bigger pan with water in it and just stir it until thickened on the spoon. Then we took it out of the pan and stirred our flavoring in it. Sometimes we used lemon, but we all liked vanilla the best. So that was dessert.

Another unusual thing we had was chestnuts. They got ripe around the first of September, just after the first frost. Then they opened up and fell to the ground, and we had lots of them, but they wouldn't last. Worms got in them right away. So we picked them up just as soon as they fell out of that hull, before the worms got to them, and took them to the house and put them, shell and all, into a two-gallon stoneware pickling jar that had a layer of salt in the bottom. We'd put about three layers of chestnuts on top of that salt, and then put another layer of salt on that and more chestnuts, and so on until it was full. Then Mother had to put a tight lid on that and hide that and put it back somewhere where we couldn't get to it because they were supposed to be saved for Christmas. One of her favorite hiding spots was back up under the stairway. We had a stair closet under there, and she'd put that jar clear back into where it'd just fit under the first two steps, you know. We were just a little afraid of that closet because once in a while we'd find a snake in there, and the mice would run in there, so she knew we wouldn't go in there after those chestnuts! But they were really good, and we would have eaten them up early if we could have got to them. Being in the shell like that, the salt wouldn't get through that shell enough to spoil them, and they'd have that nice sweet chestnutty taste. That salt was just to keep the bugs out. You know, no bug or worm will go through salt.

"From the time I was six years old on, it was all right to have a little glass of wine if we'd made it ourselves."

I guess the dandelion wine was sort of a different thing, too. From the time I was six years old on, it was all right to have a little glass of wine if we'd made it ourselves. About a year ago, I made some dandelion wine the same old way and it turn out fairly well. You get about a gallon of the yellow blossoms—pick them off right at the top of the stem—and you take two gallons of boiling water and pour that over the blossoms and add three pounds of sugar and a sliced lemon and two sliced oranges, peeling and all. Slice them up. Have all this in a big stone crock, and leave it three days. Then you strain the blossoms and everything out of it and add two or three pounds of sugar and let it sit at least nine days in a warm place. Keep a light porous cloth on top that the air can go through so it can gather that air yeast. By that time, it's just about quit going up and down [working], and then you strain it off again and put it in your bottles. Don't cork them too tight 'cause you might have an explosion! You take it and set that back in the cellar and don't even remember it's there until Christmas.

You make that in the spring, so by Christmas it's been in there about six months or more, and it's good. It's pretty strong, too! The first time I ever drank much of it, it really gave me a belt. I was about fifteen, and a cousin of mine had made a big jar of it, and he had it back in the hills in a cold spring. We were having dinner there that evening, and he asked if we'd like a glass of that wine. Of course, all of us wanted one, but I didn't know how powerful it was. It tasted like real bubbly good punch. It was just before dinner, and I was very hungry and that just tasted like real good punch. I set there, and in about half an hour that big glass of wine he gave me was all gone; and after it was all gone, why, I started to get up, but I was just a little juberous and I didn't think I could make it. So I set real still. I had drunk wine ever since I was a child, but that was the first time I had had it to hit me. The empty stomach and the high potency of the wine done the work. So anyway, I sat there, and my cousin's wife was putting the dinner on the table. She said, "I want you to sit over there." Instead of getting up and going over, I took my chair and scooted it over to the table and ate my dinner. After I ate my dinner, of course, that took the edge off of it and I was all right, but that was my first experience with really getting high. And that's about the only one! [Laughter.]

We also made strawberry wine. We had loads and loads of wild strawberries, and every spring I picked gallons of them, and Mother would put sugar on top of the berries and the juice would raise up. She didn't want that juice in her preserves anyway. She wanted her preserves kind of dry. So she always poured this juice out into the big jar, and of course she already had the sugar in it. You didn't know how much sugar really was in this juice, but if you set it in a moist temperature in the cellar and forgot about it and let it do its own thing, sometimes it made real good wine. She didn't seal it until maybe in the fall, and then she would look at it and taste it. Once in a while, if the season and the weather wasn't exactly right, it didn't work, and once in a while it would go to vinegar. But the usual thing was we had a gallon or so of just delicious strawberry wine out of the pure juice; and it was a clear and beautiful bright red wine color. I know even when I was very small, my dad used that for medicine. He always said that the Bible said that a little wine was good for your stomach, and when we would get the stomachache, Dad would always go and get us a little glass of this strawberry wine and give it to us. And if we was really sick, it *did* help. If we weren't really sick, I guess it helped, too!

My dad's birthday was December twenty-seventh, and that's when we had the more traditional, what other people had for Christmas dinner. We either had a couple of big Plymouth Rock hens, or if we'd raised enough turkeys that year and not sold them all but had saved one back for Christmas, we had turkey. We didn't like cornbread dressing, so my mother made a good biscuit dressing out of biscuits about two days old crumbled up and celery that we raised ourselves and onions and celery seeds and so on. She took the broth off the hen or the turkey and put pure broth over the bread crumbs until it was kind of gooey-like, and she stuffed the bird with this dressing, and whatever we had left over we put in a little bake pan and baked separately. All on that wood cookstove. It had a big oven with two doors that swung both ways. I'll tell you a little story about that oven. It was a cold, cold day, and Mother had left both oven doors open so the heat could come out, and we had a big old cat there, and the cat crawled up in the oven and went to sleep. Mother got ready to get dinner. Why, she shut both doors and built a fire! [Laughter.] And we heard this cat a-screaming, and we was running around the house but we couldn't find it, and we got out around the house and we came back in and we could still hear that cat a-screaming. All of a sudden, Mother thought, "It must be in the stove." She opened the stove door and here came my cat. Its paws were scorched and its hair was singed just a little bit, but the cat really wasn't hurt. But it sure never went back in that stove!

So anyway we had chicken or turkey. Up until I was twelve years old, I had to kill those chickens with an ax — put my foot on their heads and take the ax and "whang" on the chopping block! Then I plucked them and all that. After I was twelve years old, I shot them. By then I had me a .22 rifle. It was one of the first bolt-action rifles that was ever put out. A single shot. I ordered it from Sears and Roebuck. It cost $4.98. I remember that very well because I had got five dollars for hoeing corn that summer, and I paid for that rifle myself. First evening I got the rifle, I got my shells and went over the hill and killed a squirrel. Dad thought that was great.

But that first Christmas I had the rifle, Mother sent me out to kill a chicken. She had some special blue hens that were extra good layers, and then she had these Domineckers that were a whole lot bigger and better to eat, and they didn't lay like the blue ones did. She said for me to get her a big hen and, "Don't kill a blue one." So I went out and shot that Dominecker right in the head, and there was a blue one in line with the shot and it went right through its neck, and I'd killed a blue one and a Dominecker both at the same time.

I was really nervous about going in and telling her about shooting her blue hen, but Dad was in and I knew I had protection, so I said, "Oh, Mother, I shot one of your blue hens."

She said, "I thought I told you not to shoot a blue hen."

I said, "Well, I couldn't help it. It was right in line with the Dominecker. I got the Dominecker, but I've got a blue hen, too."

"Well, I reckon if you killed two birds with one stone, it's all right."

And she said, "Well, I reckon if you killed two birds with one stone, it's all right." [Laughter.]

And then, let's see, what else did we have for that dinner? Mashed potatoes. We had the baked potatoes for Christmas dinner, but for this one they were the mashed potatoes with the turkey or chicken gravy. Leather breeches beans. And we had cole slaw with that. We usually buried our cabbage in the fall in the dirt, and then if the ground wasn't froze too hard, we'd get out a head of that cabbage. And we nearly always had pickled beans and sauerkraut, and relish made out of pepper, green tomatoes, and cucumbers.

Dad wasn't great for sweets himself, but maybe we would have a spice cake—jam cake, we used to call it. We made it with jam and spices and put whipped cream on top and ate it warm.

So that was two altogether different dinners.

Missi Proffitt: One of my favorite Christmas family traditions occurs on Christmas morning every year. The day starts around 6:30 A.M. when my brother and sister jump out of their beds and fly down the stairs to see what was left for them by Santa. After checking their stockings and opening their gifts, they run through the house, first to my room to wake me up and then to my parents' room. They don't seem to understand why my parents are so slow to get out of bed, but I know. I helped them set up the things Santa brought late that night.

After we all open our presents and check our stockings, my mother and I head off to the kitchen. There we start cooking our traditional Christmas breakfast. The breakfast consists of homemade gravy, biscuits, freshly peeled and fried apples, eggs, and potatoes, and of course, a wide selection of meats: ham, bacon, sausage, turkey (from the night before), and cube steak. The table is set with the country dishes, napkins, silverware, and of course, Mom's special pick from her homemade preserves.

The first things we set out to prepare is the biscuits. We open the cabinet and find the largest bowl we can. Then we go and get the ingredients. First the flour goes in. Then the butter-flavored Crisco, and don't forget the buttermilk. To mix it all up into the dough, Mom pushes up her sleeves, and starts mixing the ingredients by hand. After she has it the way she wants it, she begins to roll the biscuits out. After getting the biscuits in the oven, she starts frying the meat. I'm peeling the apples and potatoes. I get stuck with that job every year. After all the meat is done and the apples are simmering, and the potatoes are frying, she starts on the eggs, which have to be cooked three different ways to suit the family's taste. She then starts on the gravy. She uses the grease in the skillet that the meat was fried in. She then, after getting the grease hot again, proceeds to spoon the flour in, stirring it often to get it to the right thickness. Then she pours in the milk and lets it get to a boiling point, adding salt and pepper to fit her taste. After that is made, the drinks are poured and everything set on the table. We say grace, then eat. That starts out our Christmas morning every year.

Clyde Runion: Back then you could get anything you wanted for Christmas breakfast. That's one day we got all the eggs we wanted. Through the week we didn't get many eggs.

Aunt Mo Norton: We always dressed up for Christmas dinner in the new clothes that we got. Our whole family would get together and eat lunch. Sometimes we'd invite other families from the community to come eat with us.

I first started helping my mother cook the Christmas meal when I was about eight or nine years old. The men didn't usually help cook. They would sit on the porch, or sit in the living room when it was too cold to sit out.

We always had plenty of Christmas dinner. We had our own hogs and chickens that we raised to kill and eat. We usually had ribs, fried ham, or fried chicken for Christmas dinner. We had vegetables that we'd can and put up in the summertime. We'd have beans and corn and peas. We usually had sweet potatoes because we grew our own sweet potatoes. We also grew our own Irish potatoes.

For dessert, they'd make apple pies or walnut cakes. You would just make the walnut cake like you were making any cake. Then just flour your walnuts so they won't sink to the bottom of the cake.

I still have Christmas dinner today. I have one daughter and she's got three children. They're usually here at Christmas, but if they don't come, I still have my Christmas dinner.

Aunt Nora Garland: We didn't have no cakes then because we cooked over a fireplace. But Mother'd make a great big stack of these apple pies out of dried apples, and a great big high stack of pumpkin custards. I'll never forget how she made those custards. She made hers the old-fashioned way. She'd take an egg and beat it and put in the pumpkin, the sugar, flavor, and everything, and just put all that on top of the crust. She made the crust just like any other crust—just rolled thin as it could be and put in the pan.

She'd also make four or five great big cakes of sweetbread out of our own syrup. I guess she'd put about a spoonful of ginger on it. You certainly could taste it, and good it was! We'd get a piece of that sweetbread in our stocking, too.

Icie Rickman: We'd have a dinner mostly like we do today. But instead of having turkey like we do today, we'd have chicken. We'd have chicken and gravy, dressing, potatoes, and my daddy was bad to hunt, so sometimes

105

we'd have squirrel or something like that. It was all cooked on a wood stove.

My mother made gingerbread with syrup. She put the homemade syrup with eggs, flour, ginger, and milk. To make the homemade syrup you have to plant cane in the spring out in the field. In the fall you'd cut it down. It'd grow in stalks and you'd cut it down and pile it in piles. It had what they called a head. It was a bunch thing like seeds. You'd have to cut that off. Then you'd get it stalk by stalk and pull that fodder off and pile it in another pile. It was easy. It took a long time. You'd take a big pile and you'd pull the fodder off and pile that and cut the heads off and pile them up. And then they'd gather the stalks up and put them in the wagon and take them to the cane mill to make syrup with it.

I wish y'all could see a cane mill, old timey like they used to do it. You'd put the stalks in a big old thing. They'd hook a mule up to it and he went around and around grinding that juice out of that cane. They'd put this juice in a boiler thing and cook it till it syrups.

Lassie McCall: We would always cook a lot of things, plenty to do for several days, so if company came in we'd have something sweet. Mother didn't make cakes; she made gingerbread and fruit pies maybe two days before Christmas. Of course, we were tempted to eat them. [Laughter.]

Now we didn't have what they called a pie safe, but most everybody did. My aunt had one. It had nailhead designs on a metal door. Mother just put her pies in the cupboard.

Ruby Ivie: Mama would always prepare for Christmas ahead of time by baking cakes, pies, and cookies. She would make the cookies with different shapes, real fancy like, and we'd wonder where in the world those cookies came from. We'd ask her who made those cookies, and she would say Mrs. Santa Claus. Well, we could just see Mrs. Santa Claus rolling dough and cutting cookies. Children have such good imaginations.

Burma Patterson: Till later years, we'd raise our own meats for Christmas. We'd kill hogs in November and save the backbones and ribs, and my mama'd cook a big pot of them at Christmas. They'd kill roosters and hens and make chicken and dumplings. She'd bake hams and we'd have our own homegrown meats and vegetables—Irish potatoes and sweet potatoes. We didn't have to go to the store for very much.

She'd cook a big pan of cornbread and biscuits and put clean white cloths over them, and that'd keep 'em just as moist and good.

Lilian Stiner: Christmas was a big time for us. We would make stack cakes. They would be in real thin layers and we would get dried fruit, cook it, and put it in between the layers. My mother would stack them up and put them in a high lard can. She'd close them up until Christmas. They were better—moister—after they had set awhile. Mama would bake about four or five of these cakes at Christmas if relatives were coming.

And there would be stalks of bananas hung in the closet at Christmas.

Lelia Gibson: My mother would bake five or six cakes a day or two before Christmas. Then we'd have a big cured country ham—she'd put that on to boil a day before Christmas. This ham, when it was tender and done, was skinned, and then my mother'd take black pepper, cayenne pepper, and she'd dot it all over the ham.

Leona Carver: We'd always have black walnut cake, and I still always bake about two of them. When all my children were at home, I did the cooking. Now they are married. Each family fixes something and brings it. Everybody knows what I'm going to fix. I fix the black walnut cake 'cause I know every one of them likes it.

Louise Coldren: We were fortunate enough to have apples at Christmas. They were kept in the basement all year round, and especially for Christmas. We kept our best apples until Christmas. We had worlds of chestnuts and chinquapins [at Christmas]. We had walnut, caramel, blackberry, and pound cakes, and divinity and fudge.

We started making our fruit cakes in the fall. We would soak them in apple brandy. My mother would soak it and soak it, and then take the droppings that came off one cake, and pour it over another. She liked them soaked with apple brandy.

My mother also made a sugar cookie that was just great. She would pick out the best walnuts and put them in our cookies. She would cut the cookies out and put sugar on top. It was a crisp cookie. My mother's were one of the favorites in our neighborhood.

Every fall in the Cowee
Community of Macon County,
North Carolina, neighbors
gather at the McCall farm
to grind their sorghum cane
and boil the juice down into
syrup while the children play
in the stream with toy boats.

[For Christmas dinner,] my father would be sure we would have a beef and a hog killing at Christmas. We had somebody named John Redin that would come and help us. We would kill about three hogs at one time. And we would go out at night, kill a beef, and hang it in the barn. The next morning, my daddy and I would get in the wagon, take a saw, and go from one house to another and sell pieces.

Christmas morning we usually ate late. Daddy would cook brains for breakfast. Then we would have a big dinner about two or three o'clock. Then, we would use that food for supper and eat it cold.

Gertrude Keener: I guess I might have been ten years old when I actually started cooking. The food was always in dishes that sat on the table. There was eight of us children and my daddy and mother [who] got around the table. [My mother] just cooked the dried fruit and mashed it up and rolled out her dough. [Then, she'd] put the dried apples on it and fold it over, making a moon shape, and then put it in the pan and bake it.

[To dry the apples] we had a stack, we called them, made out of wooden boards, and we cut each stack full of apples. I haven't made them in a long time, but I need to make some dried apple tarts like we used to make.

Christine Wigington: Mama always made gingerbread for us. She'd put that in our lunch boxes. It wasn't just special for Christmas, but I have that recipe and can share it with you. It's the best that anybody has ever tasted. Everybody around here has to have a piece of that gingerbread.

RECIPES

We are passing along these recipes as they have been given to us. Because they haven't been tested, some may contain errors.

Turkey Dressing

From Juanita Thurston

This recipe for our traditional Christmas dinner dressing has been passed down from my great-grandmother to my grandmother to my mom, who is telling me how to make the dressing. To make the dressing you will need the following ingredients:

12 biscuits	a pan of cornbread
2 onions	a celery stalk
pepper	turkey broth
sage	giblets

First, you take the biscuits and cornbread and crumble them up into a large bowl. Then you slice up two onions into the bowl. Next, you slice and add the celery. After that you add five dashes of pepper and a pinch of sage. Then you put in two cups of turkey broth and stir till it gets sort of smooth. Then you crush the giblets, and put them into the bowl. Stir until smooth and add three dashes of pepper and two pinches of sage. Finally, [spoon into a large baking pan and] bake it in the oven at 350 degrees for about 25 minutes.

This dish would be a tasty complement to almost any meal, especially turkey.

Cornbread Dressing

From Clyde English

cold cornbread
onion
sage

gravy from turkey or chicken
2 eggs

You take a cold [piece of] cornbread and you save your gravy that comes out when you roast your turkey or chicken. You put your gravy over the cornbread and add your onion, eggs, and sage to it. Then you bake it at 400 degrees for about 45 minutes.

Grandmother's Chicken and Dumplings

From J. D. Payne

1 large fat hen (disjointed)
flour
1 cup buttermilk

1 tablespoon salt
2 tablespoons shortening

Every Christmas when my family all gathers together to eat Christmas dinner, there is one dish that tops them all. This dish is so savory that it makes my mouth water just to think about it. It is a dish that has been prepared by my grandmother for many years. This dish is her chicken and dumplings.

In order to make this grand dish, my grandmother would get the finest hen she could find. Then she would lay the hen on the counter and cut it at the joints with a meat cleaver.

With the hen in three parts, she would put it in a five-gallon pot with a tablespoon of salt and enough water to cover the hen. Putting the pot on the stove and covering it with a lid, she would cook the hen until it was tender. After the hen was tender, she would remove it from the pot and place it aside.

Then she would take a medium-sized bowl and fill it half full of flour. With her hands, she would take two tablespoons of shortening and mix it with the flour until the flour was crumbly. Then into the bowl would go a cup of sour-smelling buttermilk. Still using her hands, she would put more flour into the bowl and mix it together. Within a few minutes, the sticky mixture would become a stiff dough. Then she would knead it lightly and roll it out into one long log. With a butcher knife she would cut the log into small pieces (about two inches long).

Next she would take the broth that was left in the pot and put the dough in it. Back onto the hot stove it would go for another twenty minutes (covered). Finally after the twenty minutes were up, she would put the chicken back into the pot to be served

In the words of my grandmother, "This is a meal that you cannot eat and sit still at the same time!"

Okra, Tomatoes, Corn, Green Peppers, and Onions

From Louise Coldren

3 cups cooked tomatoes   3 cups cooked corn
1 small green pepper   1 medium onion
10 pods small okra

Slice okra and onions in rings, dice pepper, and add to corn and tomatoes. Add salt and pepper. Cook slowly about 30 minutes. Makes 8 servings.

BREADS

Pumpkin Bread

From Louise Coldren

2½ cups flour
2 cups cooked pumpkin
½ teaspoon ground cloves
½ teaspoon salt
2 cups sugar

½ cup butter
2 teaspoons soda
½ teaspoon vanilla
1 small can evaporated milk

Mix all ingredients. Grease and flour pan. Bake at 350 degrees for 45 minutes.

Old-time Gingerbread

From Christine Wigington

½ cup Crisco
1 cup sugar
1 teaspoon soda
1 teaspoon baking powder
½ teaspoon salt
1 cup molasses or sorghum

½ cup butter
2 cups flour
1 teaspoon ground ginger
1 teaspoon cinnamon
2 eggs, beaten
1 cup boiling water

Cream butter and Crisco. Add sugar and cream until fluffy. Add eggs to butter and sugar mixture. Sift together dry ingredients and add to creamed mixture. Add molasses and mix thoroughly. Add boiling water and mix. Pour into greased and floured pan. Bake 35 to 40 minutes at 350 degrees.

Nut Bread

From Mary Pitts

4 eggs, well beaten   ½ pint (½ pound) butter
1½ cups sugar   1 teaspoon salt
1½ cups sweet milk   2 cups nuts
3 teaspoons baking powder   4 cups flour

   Combine all ingredients. Mix thoroughly. Let rise in
bread pan for 30 minutes before baking. Bake in 325-degree
oven for 45 minutes.

Banana Bread

From Beth Cranwell

1 stick butter   1 cup sugar
3 ripe bananas, mashed   3 eggs beaten until fluffy
2 cups flour   1 teaspoon baking soda
½ teaspoon salt   1 teaspoon vanilla
1 cup chopped nuts   ⅓ cup milk or orange juice

   Mix together and bake in a greased loaf pan. Bake at
350 degrees for about an hour.

Gingerbread Muffins

From Louise Coldren

¼ cup shortening	1 cup sugar
4 eggs	1 cup sorghum syrup
4 cups flour	2 teaspoons soda
2 teaspoons powdered	½ teaspoon salt
ginger	1 cup buttermilk
½ teaspoon cinnamon	

Cream shortening, add sugar, and add eggs one at a time. Mix dry ingredients. Add alternating buttermilk and syrup to first mixture. [Mix just until ingredients are combined. Overbeating will make muffins tough.] Cook in greased pan at 400 degrees for 10 to 12 minutes. Stir as little as possible. Makes 4 dozen.

CUSTARD

Holiday Boiled Custard

From Margaret Bulgin

4 cups milk	1 teaspoon vanilla
4 eggs	nutmeg
4 tablespoons sugar	

Heat the milk slowly until the steam just begins to rise over it. Beat eggs and sugar together and stir slowly into the hot milk, but do not let the mixture boil. When the mixture coats the spoon as it is lifted into the air, it is ready to be removed from the heat. Set it aside. When it cools, add vanilla. Serve with nutmeg sprinkled on top.

COOKIES

Sorghum Molasses Cookies

From Louise Coldren

1 cup brown sugar
1 cup sorghum molasses
¼ cup boiling water
flour

1 egg
¾ cup melted butter
salt

Slightly beat egg. Add sugar, sorghum molasses, butter, water, and salt. Add just enough flour to knead [into a medium stiff dough]. Roll out and cut with a cookie cutter. Bake at 400 degrees for 8 to 10 minutes. Makes 36 small cookies.

Molasses Cookies

1 stick margarine
¼ cup shortening
1 cup sugar
1 egg
¼ cup sorghum syrup
2 cups plain flour (sifted)

2 teaspoons soda
¼ teaspoon ground cloves
½ teaspoon ground ginger
1 teaspoon cinnamon
½ teaspoon salt

117

Melt and cool margarine and shortening, then add sugar, egg, and sorghum, and mix well. Add flour, soda, cloves, ginger, cinnamon, and salt. Chill overnight. Roll into 1-inch balls and roll in granulated sugar and place 2 inches apart on a greased cookie sheet. Bake 8 to 10 minutes at 375 degrees.

Gingerbread Cookies

1½ cups flour	½ cup shortening
1 teaspoon soda	½ cup brown sugar, packed
¼ teaspoon ginger	1 egg, beaten
¼ teaspoon cinnamon	½ cup molasses

Cream together the shortening and sugar. Beat in molasses and egg. Sift flour with soda, ginger, and cinnamon. Add to molasses mixture. Mix thoroughly. Turn out onto a floured surface and knead. Roll dough out and cut into cookie shapes. Bake 8 to 10 minutes on greased cookie sheet in 350-degree oven.

PIES

Grandmother's Traditional Pie

From Emma Sue Carver

My grandmother has been making this pie every year on Thanksgiving and Christmas for as long as I can remember. She is the only one in my family or anywhere that makes it as good as she does. I got this recipe from one of her recipe cards, but I had to get her to translate it for me because she had written it down so only she could read it. So here is how she told me to make it:

Combine ⅔ cup sugar, 2 tablespoons flour, 1 tablespoon cornstarch, and ¼ teaspoon salt in a heavy, deep saucepan. Gradually add 2½ cups milk to the mixture; cook on medium heat, stirring constantly. Then, beat in 3 egg yolks; add to remaining hot mixture, stirring constantly. Cook, stirring constantly, until mixture thickens. Remove from stove, and add ½ cup creamy peanut butter and ½ teaspoon vanilla extract. Stir until peanut butter melts. Add ½ cup of chocolate chips. Then pour the mixture into a baked store-bought or homemade pie crust, let it set out at room temperature for 30 minutes, and gently swirl the top of the pie with a knife to give it a "swirling water look." Then it is ready to eat. But don't eat it all in one sitting.

Pumpkin Pie

From James W. Killman

When my dad was a kid, his mom always made pumpkin pie on Christmas. She still makes it, and it's wonderful. I usually have a second helping. I called my grandmother and asked her for the recipe for pumpkin pie. She told me the recipe and I wrote it down. It is:

½ cup canned pumpkin
½ teaspoon salt
½ to 1 teaspoon ground ginger
¼ to ½ teaspoon ground cloves
1½ cups milk
9" unbaked pastry shell

¾ cup sugar
1 to 1¼ teaspoon ground cinnamon
¼ to ½ teaspoon ground nutmeg
3 slightly beaten eggs
1 (6-ounce) can evaporated milk

Combine pumpkin, sugar, salt, and spices. Blend in eggs, milk, and evaporated milk. Pour into pastry shell. Bake at 400 degrees for 50 minutes.

CAKES

Black Walnut Pound Cake

From Christine Wigington

½ pound butter	½ cup Crisco
3 cups sugar	5 eggs
5 teaspoons rum flavoring	1 teaspoon vanilla
3 cups flour	1 teaspoon baking powder
1 cup half and half cream	1 cup chopped black walnuts

Cream butter, shortening, and sugar until light and creamy. Add eggs one at a time. Beat after each egg is added. Add flavorings and beat well. Add dry ingredients alternately with cream. Lightly flour walnuts and fold into mixture. Bake in greased and floured tube pan for 80 minutes in a 325-degree oven.

Mincemeat Cake

4 cups shortening	2 teaspoons salt
6 cups sugar	4 teaspoons baking soda
1 dozen eggs	8 cups mincemeat
13 cups flour	5 cups chopped apples

Cream together shortening and sugar. Add eggs, a few at a time, beating after each addition. Sift together dry ingredients and add to creamed mixture. Mix in mincemeat and apples. Bake in two 16½" × 26" pans in a 350 degree oven for 35 to 40 minutes.

Oatmeal Cake

Wanda Cromer

The best part about Christmas is the food. Following is a recipe for a cake which I like very much that we fix at Christmastime.

1 cup oatmeal	½ cup hot water
1 stick butter, melted	1 cup brown sugar
1 cup white sugar	¼ teaspoon salt
1 teaspoon vanilla	1 teaspoon soda
1 teaspoon cinnamon	2 eggs
1½ cups self-rising flour	

Mix oatmeal and water and let stand for twenty minutes. Cream together butter, brown sugar, white sugar, and add oatmeal mixture. Add salt, vanilla, soda, cinnamon, eggs, and flour. Mix well. Bake 30 minutes at 350 degrees in a loaf pan.

Icing

1 cup brown sugar	1 cup shredded coconut
½ cup cream	1 cup chopped nuts
4 tablespoons melted butter	

Mix together and pour over hot cake. Return to oven to brown.

The Christmas Jam Cake

From Delsie Brumett

I believe the jam cake was so good because Grandma put her special love into it. Grandma gave Mom the recipe, but she just can't make the jam cake as good as Grandma did.

1 cup butter	2 teaspoons allspice
1 cup sugar	1 cup jam
3 eggs	½-1 box raisins
4 cups flour	1 cup preserves or a second
2 teaspoons soda	cup jam
2 teaspoons nutmeg	2 teaspoons cinnamon

Mix as any other cake. Bake at 400 degrees until done.

Orange Slice Cake

From Lutrelle Whiten

A long time ago, there was a little girl named Lutrelle. She had several brothers and sisters, so when Christmastime came around, she didn't get very much. Lutrelle didn't mind, as long as her mother baked an orange slice cake. She looked forward to enjoying it each and every December twenty-fifth. She liked it so much, in fact, that she baked it for her family when the time came for her to get married and settle down.

Today, to keep the tradition going, Lutrelle's only daughter (my mother) makes that delicious treat religiously. You might say that the recipe to this cake is a sacred treasure. I'd like to share it with you.

1 cup butter
2 cups sugar
1 box dates
2 cups chopped nuts
1 teaspoon of soda (dissolved in ½ cup of buttermilk)

4 eggs
3½ cups plain flour
1 box or can flaked coconut
1 package orange slice candy

Cream butter and sugar. Add eggs one at a time. Add flour alternately with milk. Roll nuts, orange slice candy, and dates in flour. Add with coconut to batter. Bake in tube pan at 250 degrees for 2 to 2½ hours.

Orange Sauce

1 cup orange juice   2 cups powdered sugar

Mix well, and pour over cake as soon as taken from oven. (Let cake stand in pan overnight.)

Apple Stack Cake

From Vadie Barron

3 eggs
1½ cups sugar
   flour to thicken mix

1½ cups milk
2 teaspoons vanilla

Mix together all ingredients, pour into a pan, and bake for 30 minutes. Bake 3 layers.

Use 1 quart jar sour apples. Take canned apples, put in pan, and heat on high for 20 minutes.

Use 1 cup of sugar to sweeten apples, and ½ teaspoon cinnamon for flavor. Mix ingredients.

Take first layer of cake and spread apples over it.

Take second layer of cake and spread apples over it.

Take third layer of cake and spread apples over it.

CANDY

Peanut Butter Fudge

From Virginia Gail Reynolds

½ cup butter or margarine
1 pound light brown sugar
½ cup milk
¾ cup smooth or crunchy
    peanut butter

1 teaspoon vanilla extract
1 pound confectioners sugar

In medium saucepan, melt butter; stir in brown sugar and milk. Bring to a boil; boil and stir 2 minutes. Remove from heat; stir in peanut butter and vanilla. Mix in confectioners sugar; beat until smooth. Spread into buttered 9-inch square baking pan. Chill until firm. Cut into squares. Makes 3½ pounds.

Snowy White Fudge

From Virginia Gail Reynolds

3 cups sugar
1 (5-ounce) can evaporated milk
1 (7-ounce) jar marshmallow creme

½ cup (1 stick) butter
1 cup chopped walnuts
1 teaspoon vanilla

In heavy saucepan, combine sugar, butter, and milk. Bring to a rolling boil over medium heat, whisking constantly to prevent scorching. Continue for 5 minutes. Remove from heat; add marshmallow creme and stir until smooth. Add walnuts and vanilla and stir until blended. Pour into a buttered, 8-inch square pan. Place pan on wire rack to cool; cut into squares. Makes about three pounds.

Fudge Candy

From Mary Pitts

4 cups sugar
2 cups sweet milk
chopped nuts (optional)

1 lump of butter the size of a walnut
4 tablespoons cocoa

Boil sugar and sweet milk until it reaches candy stage. This can be checked by dropping a small amount into cold water, and when it forms a ball, remove from heat. Add butter, cocoa, and nuts and beat until thick enough to cut. Pour into buttered pan or dish and let set until hard.

Popcorn Balls

From Lessie Conner

In order to make the popcorn balls, a large iron skillet is needed, along with two large dishpans or bowls (one for the popped corn and one for the finished popcorn balls), one mixing bowl for the cooked syrup, and several kitchen spoons.

To make the syrup for the popcorn balls, pour a quart of sorghum in the large iron skillet to heat on the stove. The reason for the large skillet is that the syrup boils up, and the reason for an iron one is that it heats evenly and will not burn the syrup as readily as another type of pan.

Lessie Conner making popcorn balls.

You can tell when the syrup is ready because it forms a "hair" when dripped down from the spoon. When the syrup gets to the stage where the hair will drop off the spoon, it is ready. It will take about five minutes to get to that stage. Pour the syrup into the mixing bowl to cool for several minutes. It should come right off the heat and preferably right out of the pan when it's completely cooked, or it will get brittle when it cools. Cover your hands with butter to keep the syrup from sticking to them while forming the balls. It is better to use cold rather than warm popcorn, because the syrup will stick better.

There are two methods for forming the popcorn balls. The first method is to carefully place a small amount of popcorn into the palm of one hand and carefully (because the syrup could still burn) spoon about a tablespoon of syrup on top of it. Then pack the popcorn and syrup mixture together by hand. Use additional butter on your hands after making a few balls or the syrup will start sticking to them.

The second method is to add one or two teaspoons of baking soda to the syrup while it is boiling. The soda makes the syrup bubble and foam up, giving more candy to work with. Then pour the syrup into the mixing bowl, and on top of that pour the popcorn. Stir that up with a wooden spoon and scoop it out with your hands to form the balls. After each popcorn ball is made, place it in a large dishpan or on waxed paper to cool.

Divinity

From Mary Pitts

2⅓ cups sugar
⅔ cup white Karo syrup
½ cup water
½ cup chopped black walnuts (optional)

¼ teaspoon salt
2 egg whites, beaten stiff
½ teaspoon vanilla

Combine sugar, Karo syrup, water, and salt in a saucepan. Bring to a boil and cook until it "spins a thread." That's when you pull the mixture up with a spoon and it forms little hairs. When the syrup mixture spins a thread, pour about half of it into the beaten egg whites, beating it constantly.

Bring the other half of the syrup mixture back to a boil, because it will have cooled off. Then slowly beat this half of the mixture into the egg whites. Add vanilla. Keep beating until it is thick enough to form a piece of candy with a spoon. Spoon out onto waxed paper in tablespoon-sized pieces and let harden. (A half cup of chopped black walnuts may be added to the candy mixture when the vanilla is added, if desired.)

Syrup Candy

From Lessie Conner

1 cup sorghum   1 cup water
dash of salt

Combine all ingredients and boil (do not stir) until it reaches the hard-ball stage. [When a small amount of the mixture forms a hard ball when dropped into water, it is ready.] Remove from the heat and let it stand until cool enough to hold in well-greased hands. Using a small amount at a time, pull the candy back and forth between the hands. After pulling for some time, it will change from a brown to a yellowish color, at which time it is ready to eat.

Penuche

From Gail McCurry

4 cups of brown sugar   1 cup evaporated milk
1 tablespoon of butter   1 tablespoon of Karo syrup
1 cup chopped walnuts

Cook sugar, butter, milk, and syrup over medium heat, stirring constantly until it comes to a boil. At first sign of bubbles, count five minutes of boiling. Remove from heat immediately.

Beat with electric beaters until creamy and smooth. Add cup of chopped walnuts and stir to combine. Spread in greased 7" × 10" × 1½" pan. Let harden. Cut into squares. Store in airtight container.

FIVE
Other Traditions

Edited by Chuck Clay and Anthony Queen

"Come on, hurry up. We've got to go sparking at Bass's house. There's going to be candy pulling, singing, the whole bit! The whole family is coming up and should be here by dark, if the train's on time. Better put a backstick in the fireplace before we go."

Sound crazy? Well, those are just a few of the many traditions celebrated by people of this region. Hunting for rabbits or hogs on Christmas day was very common. For fun, children slid down hills covered with fresh white powder on wooden sleds made by their fathers or older brothers. As a family, going to find that special tree was always a part of Christmas. If you were the outgoing type of person who enjoyed having something to do all the time, you wouldn't find Christmas back then one bit boring. There was constantly a square dance at somebody's house with the furniture moved aside to make room. Across this mountain region people played games like "pleased or displeased" and "crossed questions or crooked answers." They also attended special church services where the preacher might play Santa Claus and hand out gifts.

In this chapter, people discuss individual traditions celebrated by their families that are in addition to those already included in this book. Some would have a backstick in the fireplace so large that it would last three days. Other people would take the bladders out of the hogs they killed and use them as balloons. People would bake a big loaf of bread with a dime in it. Whoever got the dime had good luck for a whole year.

We still have traditions today but the traditions have changed, as you will see. As long as families celebrate Christmas together, however, there will always be Christmas traditions.

—Chuck Clay

"There was always a lot of devilment goin' on."
Ethel Corn

Ethel Corn greeted us at the door of her house trailer with a big, friendly smile and began telling us about her

132

Christmases as a child almost before we could get the tape recorder plugged in!

As she talked, she pointed out her window to her quarter-acre garden spot, showing us plants already peeking up. She often turned the conversation for a chance to talk about her pride in the fact that she gardens alone, completely by hand. From Mrs. Corn's living room window, one can also see the old, two-story log cabin in which she was born about eighty years ago. It was here that Ethel was raised to a young woman, later returning to live out the rest of her life.

Ethel Corn: I can't hardly tell you my favorite part of Christmas. I loved every minute because that was the day our Savior was borned on.

We'd decorate the house with cedar and holly, and my daddy would generally get the Christmas tree. We've had trees here that would touch the ceiling. We would make decorations with different colored paper—link chains—and with popcorn and pine cones. Back then, there was no electrical power, and we used candles with clamps on the bottom. One time, one of those candles got too hot and them needles caught on fire, and I never did put another up on a tree.

We would get these sycamore balls and paint them all different colors and they made pretty decorations. For snow, I'd take wash powders and add some water and beat them with an egg beater. Just beat a foam out of it and put that all over the Christmas tree like snow. It would stay there for three or four days.

Ethel Corn.

On Christmas Eve night, they'd have a Bible play at the church, and we'd go caroling and sing and have fun. Then we'd have candy drawings. Someone would buy stick candy and break it up, mix it all up, all different colors, and we young people would choose up partners. If you and your partner didn't draw the same color of candy, you'd put it back. If we did draw the same color, we'd keep it. We'd do that until all the candy was gone.

I never knowed Dad to work on Christmas Day. He'd just take that one day off from the farm. The family was always together at Christmas.

For Christmas dinner, we'd have turkey and ham and vegetables to go with it, and every kind of cake that could be imagined nearly. My mother always baked gingerbread, and we had cookies and candies and oranges and apples, and all kinds of nuts. We'd get into the candy and get all that stuff and go to eatin'. That was generally the rule at Christmas when we was little. There was always a lot of devilment goin' on.

I believe that they do wrong in having them big dinners and so much to eat on Christmas. Nearly everybody will eat a way too much and they'll be sick. It used to be after Christmas, there'd be a doctor bill to pay, and I don't believe people ought to cook like that and serve that much food. I tell you, our body, the Bible tells us, is God's temple, and if we eat too much, it'll hurt us, and then we're defiling God's temple!

When it snowed, we'd go out and play in the snow and we'd get a whippin'! We'd just get anything that we could slide on and made sleds, ride on that sled. Oh, I can remember that there used to be a barn set up yonder on the hill, and there was a slope from up there to down to the back of Lucy's place over there. Me and my brother would get up there and sit on boards about six inches wide and come way down here—just wear the seat out of our clothes! Mama would warn us about gettin' out, and she'd tell us to stay in on account of making us sick, but quick as her back was turned, we would slip out! Somehow or 'nother, we just couldn't resist that.

[As I got older,] I hated to see a white Christmas because the old people always said, "A white Christmas for a fat graveyard." I don't know if there was anything to this, but there'd be a lot of deaths during the year [following a white Christmas]. It seemed like it worked out that way.

People buy toys every week nearly nowadays. Every time they go to the store, a young 'un gets a toy, but they don't enjoy it. They just play with it for a few weeks and then it's tore up. But when Christmas came, if they didn't get toys all year 'round, they'd like it a whole lot better. They get so many, they don't hardly enjoy it. Christmastime was the only time we got toys and all things like that. There's a lot of difference in the way it was then and the way it is now.

Billy and Annie Long: We used to play games. We'd have candy drawings when we'd all get together. It was planned ahead of time. We'd buy two or three boxes of stick candy, different colors. We'd break it up, put it in a dishpan, and mix it all together. Somebody'd sit in here with a cloth over the dishpan. You'd have to run your hand in there, and you couldn't see what you was getting. We were all coupled up. We'd always let the girls draw, and then we boys would try to match our girlfriend's. If you got one like hers, you got to keep it. If you didn't, you had to put it back and go on. We'd just keep doing that until we'd get that candy all drawed out of there. Sometimes we'd put in two or three hours. It was fun. We enjoyed it.

Aunt Mo and Tommy Lee Norton: When there was a dance, our parents would let us stay out until 12 A.M. The kind of dancing we did was square dancing. That was all we knew how to do. We didn't dress up for our dances, we just wore anything we had.

Usually we had somebody who would play all the time for the dances. We would go in and move everything out of the way. Then after we were finished, we would put everything back.

We always went rabbit hunting on Christmas or the day before Christmas. The hunting trip would be all day long. That was the thing to do. We'd have brothers, brothers-in-law, and friends that would go. I didn't eat the rabbit, though, I don't like rabbit.

Aunt Mo and
Tommy Lee Norton.

Douglas Jump: As for decorations and ornaments, every family member would select or make an ornament for the tree which represented something that had happened to them during the year. The males in the family always went out and selected a tree on Christmas Eve day, and everyone would help decorate it.

Randy Love: One of the traditions [my grandmother, Mrs. Joe Love] remembers most when she was young was that the tree had decorations made by hand. The only decoration not made by their hands was the popcorn that they strung. She felt that the popcorn was made by God, and they were putting it to use on the tree that symbolized Jesus Christ coming into this world.

137

Bass and Lucy Hyatt: After I got big enough to spark, we went to dances. Sometimes they'd have them on New Year's Eve. Had them at people's houses, you know. We'd have corn shuckings, and then that night we'd have a big dance at the house. Maybe a candy pulling or a candy breaking. People got their corn gathered and their fall work done, and everybody in the community would get together at somebody's house. They would give us a room to have a dance in. They'd have plenty of 'em to make music. They'd take time about playing instruments and then dancing. Everybody would ride out to the farm where the dance was, tie their horses up out there. And some would come in a buggy, maybe. We'd sit up and wait for New Year's.

"The houses were small, and some people did not have a living room they could dance in, but we would take the bed down."

Louise Coldren: The houses were small, and some people did not have a living room they could dance in, but we would take the bed down. They would have a fiddler, and after each set we put a nickel or dime in the hat to pay the fiddler. We had wonderful music, and we danced and had a great time.

There was always refreshments at everybody's house: cakes, cider, or hot chocolate. We sometimes would have a sack full of candy. Then a boy would reach downward, get a piece. If he got the same kind of candy that the girl had picked, then they could take a walk together.

When it snowed, thirty to forty people came and

brought their sleds over to go sledding. The men and boys made our sleds. The snow on the ground would freeze, and we would slide on that. We would sled all night long by firelight. We would come home, dry our clothes, and go back out.

Burma Patterson: Now I *mean* we had good parties. We'd have a party just about every weekend either at our house or at some friend's house. We had a little living room, but we had a big bedroom. My daddy would let us move the beds out on a Saturday night, and we'd have a little square dance as we got grown. And he was a music master! He could play the organ, play the fiddle, pick the guitar and the banjo. He could make any kind of music — and just by ear. He could make an instrument talk. He loved to have his friends come and play for us to dance.

We had games we'd play, too. We'd play "pleased or displeased" and we'd play "crossed questions or crooked answers." That's so funny. You line up a bunch of girls on one side and a bunch of boys on the other, and three people tell *them* separately what they're supposed to ask and answer. Neither one of those three know what the others said. We usually got a man to tell the boys something. They might ask, "Will you marry me?" Well, no one else knew what the boy was going to ask the girl, and the girls had answers they were supposed to give like, "Come see me sometime," or "I'll meet you at the wash place" [the creek or branch where the clothes were washed].

My mother had cakes baked, and she made the chil-
dren hot chocolate. Young folks didn't drink coffee back then, but she had coffee for the older ones who might want it. She would line us up around the table and let the girls

feed their boyfriends—give them a bite of cake. Then the boys fed cake to their girlfriends and gave them a sip of cocoa, and it was fun!

Doris Shumate: We danced a lot the night before Christmas. I played the guitar and Herman played the fiddle. Then we had a blind boy, my sister's boy. He played everything. He played the banjo, guitar, and the fiddle. Honey, he could tune one and pick up the other and tune it with that one. He could play the French harp. He was a genius, I tell you. My whole family sings. Thank the Lord, they all get along. They sing good.

Bass and Lucy Hyatt: We had relatives and neighbors who had moved away come back to celebrate Christmas with us. There was lots of people who went to Texas about eighty, ninety years ago. They bought land there, got land cheap. They got into wheat farming and raising cattle, and they made money; they done well. Then they'd come back here about every Christmas, you know. They'd get a round-trip ticket on the train back then for about fifteen or twenty dollars. Then after Christmas, they'd go back home. The train came to Murphy [North Carolina] back as far as I can remember.

Ada Kelly: Several relatives in the family that lived away would visit for a whole week during Christmas holidays, and that was a week we always looked forward to. We had time to visit then. We had to walk or go horseback or in the wagon. Early in my life, a lot of the wagons were drawn by oxen. My father had a team of horses from the beginning, but the majority of people had oxen hitched to their wagons, and for long years that was the custom.

Lassie McCall: In third grade, my teacher, James Keener, had big Christmas programs. We called him "Teacher Jim," and he had beautiful Christmas celebrations. He would turn us out of a day and we'd all go to the mountains and gather in greenery to decorate with. We got a tree, also. We'd come back, and when that big stove [heated with wood] got hot, that pine would smell so good. Teacher Jim would let us pull up those benches or pews (see, school was in the church) and gather around the heater so we could be warmer. I can remember that still yet. He always had a program with recitations. It was always something pertaining to Christmas and stressed the religious part of it. There might be some humor in there, too, but it was largely religious. He always invited parents in, too, and a good many people would come. That was sort of the highlight of the community.

Everybody took Christmas off. We wouldn't have to work around the farm. Usually our dad would specially get some wood up ready for good big fires. He would always get what he called a backstick, a big log to put in the fireplace, and it would last about three days. I guess it was called a Yule log in England. Dad just called it a backstick.

Mattie Pearl McGaha: I can remember my daddy talking about how they used to soak a log in the branch [stream] and get it wet. And that was called our backstick. And they would put it on, and as long as it didn't burn up, then they got to celebrate Christmas, and they wouldn't have to work.

Icie Rickman: I still don't take my tree down till after New Year's. They say it's bad luck. A lot of people do that; they're superstitious. But it's just an old saying.

Gertrude Keener: We would help put on a Christmas play at church. We dressed the children up in paper dresses. We made their little costumes out of crepe paper. We'd decorate them and dress them up, and they would have a little cloak on. And we'd read just a little verse from the Bible. We usually read the Christmas story.

Nearly every Christmas, my daddy would go wild turkey hunting. We had a lot of wild turkeys in the woods when we were younger, and we'd see him come back through the fields with a big turkey on his back. We were just tickled to death. And my mother would cut the tips of the wings off, and the tail, and put a smoothing iron on them and dry them out for fans to fan the fire with.

Mary Ann Hollifield: We would sit around the fire at night, of course. The fireplace was the only heat we had for the house, and we would sit around it. We would get a lot of rich pine, you know, and then get the fire to blazing. Then my mom and dad would tell us stories about Christmas and Christ's birthday and why we had it. We enjoyed that, of course.

Douglas Jump: Each year, every family member would make up a song about another family member. On Christmas Eve, after opening all the gifts, each member would

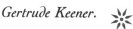
Gertrude Keener.

sing his song. Every member of the family has a collection of songs that have been written about him.

Ruby Ivie: We would wear that little saying, "Christmas gift," out every time. We would say to each other, "Christmas gift!" So they would have to run and get a piece of candy, an orange, or an apple. Everybody said it to each other all the time on Christmas Day. Sometimes we would say "Christmas Eve Gift," and let us know it wasn't time to have "Christmas gift." It lasted only one day, but as I remember it was a jolly good time.

Ida Neal: The thing I enjoyed the most was when you saw your neighbor. You would always try to see them before they saw you, because whoever said "Christmas Gift!" first, received a gift from that neighbor.

Leo Bradley Gibson: We'd go to the chinquapin orchard on Sunday and get chinquapins. One time I think I strung four hundred and wore them around my neck to school. There was four strings and they hung down to my knees. The boys would grab the chinquapins, you know, and take them off the string and bite them in two. Chinquapins are something like a chestnut, only smaller. They are like beads [and] taste like chestnuts.

Aaron Miller: On Christmas Day my grandma bakes a big loaf of bread with a dime in it. Then everybody takes off a piece of bread, and if you get the dime, you have good luck for a whole year.

SIX
Stories

Edited by Rabun Baldwin

So far in this book, you have read chapters about ingenious ways of making Christmas gifts, delicious recipes, humorous stories of serenading, and much more. Many of these chapters contained stories: stories about the time people realized there was really no Santa Claus, and about the practical jokes people played on each other on Christmas Eve.

Those were just a few of the stories people shared with us. The following stories do not belong in any of the previous chapters—they have a special quality, and some are so unusual we felt they needed a chapter of their own. The stories in this chapter range from being funny, like the

story about some plum pudding and a little package of powdered sauce—they thought! Or they are even sad, like the
following story of Carolyn Stradley and how she spent
Christmas alone.

—Rabun Baldwin

"It was Christmas day, and I felt very much alone."
Carolyn Stradley

At eleven years old, Carolyn Jones was living alone in
the mountains of northeast Georgia. Her mother had died,
and her father had abandoned her.

At the age of thirteen, she packed up her few belong-
ings and caught a ride to Atlanta. There she rented a small
garage apartment with her brother, enrolled herself in a
nearby high school, and got a job at the local Howard
Johnson's. Two years after her move to Atlanta, Carolyn
met and married Arthur Stradley. When she became preg-
nant during her junior year of high school, she left school.
After her daughter, Tina, was born, she returned to night
school to complete her education. She got a job as a secre-
tary with a paving company and worked her way up to a
management position. As she progressed, the company of-
fered to pay her tuition toward a certificate in civil engi-
neering from Georgia Tech.

When Carolyn had advanced in the paving company
to a point where she felt she could go no higher, she left it.
She, her brother, and his wife, Shirley, got a loan and

started their own paving business. Thus began C & S (standing for Carolyn and Shirley) Paving Company, which she now runs. C & S Paving recently contracted to do some of the paving of the new runways at the Hartsfield International Airport in Atlanta.

Mrs. Stradley stands about five feet, eight inches tall. A very friendly, attractive woman, she has thick, wavy, shoulder-length red hair and freckled skin, and her bright blue eyes are edged with laugh lines. This story she tells of her childhood in the mountains is one of the most powerful we have ever collected.

—Patsy Singleton, Allison Adams, and Eddie Kelly

Carolyn Stradley: I was born in 1946 in the small community of Youngcane, which is in Union County, near Blairsville, in the mountains of northeastern Georgia. That's where I was raised until I was thirteen [except for times when we moved to Atlanta for short periods.]

My childhood was probably just typical of the area. There was a garden, and we canned what we grew. We dried leather breeches beans. All my life, I can't remember *not* being responsible for someone or something. Even as a small child, it was my responsibility to make sure there was water in the house. I went up to the spring and brought in water, carried in wood, and made sure that the chickens had been fed. These were all things that were necessary.

I started grammar school out at the old Blairsville school [about 1952]. Our school bus was a pickup truck with a wooden cover on the back and little wooden benches. And if it rained real bad, then we didn't go to school because the roads were so bad that the little truck couldn't get across the creeks. This was in the fifties, but very few people in our area had automobiles and the roads were terrible!

In the sixth and seventh grades, I was going to school over there at Youngcane. I can remember we did not even have electricity at home at that particular time. We were still using a kerosene lamp. When I first got into geometry in the seventh grade, it was very difficult at nights sitting by a kerosene lamp trying to get my geometry homework.

Daddy worked in a sawmill and did a little moonshining, and he hauled produce into Atlanta. Mother never worked outside the home. She was often extremely sick. As a child, I can remember her being in the hospital a lot. She had had rheumatic fever and she developed heart disease. She would get out and work like a man, though. She would do sawmilling with my father and pull a crosscut saw. Then she'd get really sick! [She died when] I was eleven. I believe I was in the sixth grade.

She had been a very strong, independent person. She had grown to be that way with Daddy's habits of coming in one week and gone the next. There was never anything she could depend on.

First of all, please understand that I loved my father more than anything else in the world, but Daddy was an alcoholic. My mother died on a Sunday, she was buried on Tuesday, and the following weekend, my father was remarried. He chose to live in the Atlanta area with his new wife. [He left my brother and me in our little house in Youngcane to look after ourselves.]

My brother, Eldon, is four years older than I. His responsibilities were similar to mine. A lot of times he would do what they called "off-bearing" in a sawmill. Off-bearing is where someone catches the slabs that come off the side of the tree trunk whenever a tree is run through the saw. They'd catch those slabs and lay them somewhere else. Even though he was a young boy, he was very strong and he would do that a lot of times for his money. Eldon worked at the sawmill or cleaned out chicken houses — things like that. Whatever he could pick up. He would come in and live with me part of the time between jobs.

Mother had managed to get the house paid off before she died. There wasn't much to it, but it was shelter. The winters get sort of severe there, and I can remember waking up sometimes and I'd have ice frozen across my face from the condensation of my breath. I think being cold was one of the things I remember most. It would be dark by the time the school bus got me home. Some mornings I didn't properly cover the coals in the fireplace before I left for school and I would come in by myself in the evening and not have kerosene to start a new fire. I'd have to get a new fire going in the dark.

Bobby socks were the popular thing at that time, and I only had one pair. I'd wash them, and if they weren't dry by the next morning, I'd put them on wet. I think being laughed at and made fun of in school and never feeling like I was as good as anyone else were probably the worst things. When I was in the seventh grade, one of the things that I really remember most of all was this girl giving me a bar of soap for Christmas. Of course she was trying to be obnoxious, because she knew I had never had anything like that. [We made lye soap instead.] She didn't realize that was the best Christmas present I had. It was probably the only Christmas present I had that year. Surviving was a day-in, day-out process. I had learned to can vegetables and dry beans and dry apples and fix kraut, so most of the time I had enough canned [food to last me]. I wore a lot of my brother's clothes, hand-me-downs. I worked hard through the summertime and usually would get enough money to buy enough clothes to just about last through the winter. Farmers in that area grew vegetables for the big food companies like Campbell Soup and Stokely. They sent big open trucks along the country roads to pick up people who wanted to work by picking the beans, peppers, or whatever in the summertime. In the mornings, just at daybreak, big trucks came along near where I lived and picked us up and carried us to the fields, and we would be in the fields all day. It might be where they'd be cutting cabbage and loading them into a sled, or they might be picking peppers. But mainly the thing that I did was pick beans because I was not fast enough to make any money the other ways. But beans—I learned to pick those quite well. I could make a quarter a bushel picking beans!

Also, I would keep people's children for them. I'd also take in laundry. Of course, up there you had to either go to the creek or the spring to get water, or draw up water if you were fortunate enough to have a well. And you either had a rub board or, again, if you were fortunate, you had the old-fashioned wringer washing machine. I had a rub board.

Then, whenever school was in, I really had it made because I got one good hot meal a day. At school there was a long noontime recess, and I would sweep the floors in the school at that time, and then wash dishes. That way I could have all I wanted to eat. That was how I got through the week.

I never begged. I never begged and I never had the first welfare check. And I never stole anything to eat. I'd wash dishes, or I'd watch a kid, or I'd mop floors, or wash windows, or whatever was necessary. I've never been ashamed of doing anything to make money that was honest and that I felt good about. And I've tried to do [every job] to the best of my ability.

To some degree, I enjoyed my life in the mountains. The fact that I felt independent, the fact that I could card wool and could make a medicine out of herbs, could heat resin out of a pine knot to close a wound, made it almost enjoyable. These were things that I lived with day in and day out. I never felt that that was bad. I just felt a lot of emotional conflicts inside with the loneliness. That was the worst feeling. Being alone; never really feeling like I belonged. If I went to someone's house and they had children of their own, I felt like I was invading them.

One particular Christmas—I guess I was eleven—I had been by myself. Dad was down in the city with his friends and Eldon was away. I had got a Christmas tree, and at school we'd colored little strips of paper and glued them into chains for decorations.

It was Christmas Day, and I felt very much alone. I didn't want to spend Christmas that way. I had a girlfriend who was the preacher's daughter, so I thought, "Well, it's Christmas Day and there's going to be good spirit and good cheer at the preacher's house." It was spitting snow—not the pretty snow but the old slushy, sloppy, sleet-type stuff— but I walked down across the field and started to cross the creek on the foot log. Just as I was crossing it, I slipped and fell in the creek, just like a kid will. But I got out and walked on up through another field to his house.

When I first went in, I didn't feel any kind of uncomfortableness. They had a big fire built, and their house was so nice and warm, and I was cold and I was wet. So I went behind the heater to dry out.

They were cooking, and there were all these fragrances in the house, and I had not eaten at all, so the smells of the turkey and sage dressing and all that food had my mouth watering.

And so we sat there for a while and visited, and then the preacher's wife came in and said, "We're ready to eat!" And all the family went into the dining room. I stood back because out in the country, there's sort of an unwritten code that you never go to anyone's table unless you're asked. You just don't do it. And so I waited a few minutes, and the preacher came back and pulled me aside and said, "Carolyn, I don't get to spend very much time with my family alone. Why don't you come back later?"

He didn't say, "Would you leave?" But I knew what he meant. At eleven years old, I looked at it like, "What did I do wrong? Yes, I tracked some mud on the floor, and I'm sorry, and I cleaned it up," but I didn't know what else it was that I had done wrong.

And so I left. And I didn't go back. And even now, I resent anyone that even looks like him. I haven't been strong enough to find forgiveness or forgetting inside of me for what he did. I've had drunk guys in Atlanta come and try to rape me, and I've fought them off with a butcher knife, and I don't hate *them* the way I hate that preacher, because they never professed to be loving and gentle and kind and then turn around and turn someone away who just wanted something to eat.

And from that day on, I vowed that I would never allow that to happen to me again. I vowed that I would never beg for anything from anyone else for as long as I live. I'm still pretty strict about that. If I can't get something I want by myself, then in my mind I won't let myself want it, if you understand what I mean. I have found that to survive in this world, you have to ask for some things, but you don't have to beg for anything. I haven't, and with God's help, I won't. I'll beg God for help and forgiveness, but not another human being.

Another result of that experience is that when I prepare food for Christmas, I cook for twenty people when only three are coming! If the local football team dropped in at my house, there'd be plenty of food for them. And I get paranoid if I get low on groceries. After my husband died, when it was only my daughter and me at home, I would still have two refrigerators and a freezer full of food, plus canned goods. I never ever wanted her to experience this feeling of hunger, of being cold, of fear, or being alone, and of rejection.

Of course, there were good Christmases when I was young. When Mom was alive, one year I remember my brother had a BB gun on layaway and I had a doll on layaway. I can remember the cost of the doll. It was five dollars. And once a month we would go in the store and she would pay fifty cents on that doll. And whenever she made a payment, they would get this doll down off the shelf and I got to sit there and hold it. I knew that if I was a good little girl, then Santa Claus would bring me that doll for Christmas. That was one of the best Christmases that I remember—when Santa *did* bring me that doll, and he brought my brother the BB gun.

Lucille Ponder: When we went to my grandma's on Christmas, we went in what they called a jolt wagon. And if it was cold, they'd put a lantern to their feet and put a quilt up over that. And they'd fix us kids in the back of the wagon. They'd put hay down, put a quilt over that, and then a quilt over us. We'd lay down in the wagon bed, and we'd stay warm.

Edith Cannon: I love Christmas songs. We always sang lots of Christmas songs about a month before Christmas. So one summer, in the middle of the summer, we were invited over at King Memorial Church for some special day. So our pastor asked if anybody had a special song that they wanted sung. My son, Stephen, selected a Christmas song. Well, that kind of tickled everybody. The pastor says, "No sir, son, that's all right. The songs are wonderful to sing all during the year if you want to."

Marie Tudor: Once I was being punished, as usual, for something I can't quite remember. My mother was keeping me in the closet near the kitchen where she was working. Feeling sorry for myself, I was sniffling. In the middle of a sniff, I noticed a very pleasant smell—oranges! It was nearly Christmas, and my mother had hidden the fruit that we children would get in our stockings in that closet! I just had to have a taste, and then another. My mother would call to me, "Marie, have you learned your lesson? Are you ready to come out and behave yourself?" My reply was, "No, ma'am," and I would eat another piece of fruit. By the time she caught on to what I was doing, I was ready for a big dose of soda water!

Nicole Skeen: When [my grandmother, Lula Skeen,] was eight, her sister Mary Jane made a caramel cake a couple days before Christmas. My grandmother kept pinching off pieces of the icing, and when her sister would ask her about it, she would deny doing it and swear it was a little mouse!

Louise Hooper: We lived in a country house with a kitchen and a dining room. You had to go out of the living room on the back porch to go into the dining room and the kitchen. My mother kept the candy, nuts, and fruit stuck away in the dining closet. One Christmas morning [when] she was in there cooking breakfast, my sister and I got into the goodies! My mother caught us, and she sent Daddy to give us a whipping.

"Daddy didn't have the heart to spank us. He said, 'Okay now, girls, I'm not gonna spank you, but you'd better holler real big and loud so that she'll think I'm really spanking you hard.'"

Daddy didn't have the heart to spank us. He said, "Okay now, girls, I'm not gonna spank you, but you'd better holler real big and loud so that she'll think I'm really spanking you hard." So we did. We hollered and carried on, but we weren't really getting spanked at all.

D. B. Dayton: My mom and dad got along the best you ever seen till Christmas. Daddy'd get drunk ever' Christmas. He worked like a slave, though, all the rest of the time. When Christmas come, we'd have two peppermint sticks, an orange, and an apple in our stockings. That's what we'd have.

My daddy went off to the store one time, and he got our Christmas [gifts] that day, and he got him a new pair of overalls. Somebody gave him some liquor (he couldn't buy it), but somebody gave him enough to get him drunk. He walked home. It's four miles from town to where we live, and when we seen him coming, Mommy says, "He's drunk." She could tell just as well. We went out to meet him. He had a box of candy and one leg of those new overalls under his arm. The other leg of 'em was dragging in the dirt. He had that candy strowed everywhere. We went back down the road and picked up the sticks of candy where he split it—them long, hard sticks of peppermint.

When he got home, Mommy got on him. Just as sure as he got drunk, she'd get on him right then, and make it worse. If she'd just a-waited till he got sober, it'd been a whole lot better, but she'd get on him and they'd quarrel. They'd have a cuss fight just as sure as he'd get drunk. They wasn't a Christmas that passed that he didn't get drunk, but through the other times, he hardly ever did.

Bill Robertson: My brother, Henry, told me that Santa was going to come see him twice. I was old enough not to believe in Santa, so I knew better. We made a bet that if he did, Henry would win my new 1916 quarter, and if I won, I would get his. I went ahead and ate my fruit and candy because those were the only nicknacks we got all year. Henry hid his away, and I knew it.

I heard Henry get up out of bed that night and put his candy back in his stocking. After he came back to bed and went to sleep, I got up and ate his candy and fruit! I got double the nicknacks and another quarter.

Louise Coldren: My mother's village was in Horse Cove. That is where the Chatooga River begins. An English family came and they lived there for about five or six years. Then they decided to go back to England. In the meantime, one of the girls had married a cousin of mine. At Christmas time, she always got a package from home. They would send baby clothes, blankets, and one of the things her mother would always send was plum pudding. This particular year the plum pudding came, and a small package came with it. Well, she thought that it was sauce to go over the pudding, so she mixed it with sugar and water and poured it over the plum pudding.

When she wrote her mother and thanked her, she told her they did not like the sauce and had to scrape it off. When her mother wrote back, she said, "Oh, I forgot to tell you Uncle Harry died. We had him cremated and those were his ashes. He wanted to be put in the Chattooga River."

Robert Ricker: The funniest Christmas story [my mother, Doris Ricker,] remembered was when her Uncle Kenneth put a humongous gift box underneath the tree for her grandmother. Her grandmother could not wait to open the present because she thought she was going to get a recliner. When she opened the box, there was a smaller

157

box inside, then another smaller box, then another, and another. When her grandmother finally got to the end, there was a tiny box. Inside the box was a pig's tail with a ribbon tied around it. My mom and her family got a real kick over this episode.

Gail Hepburn: One Christmas, Irene [Galyon's] twin sister and she had gotten some beads just alike. She broke hers in the summer. When she was stringing the beads back following the pattern of Irene's necklace, she noticed a blue bead missing. Her brother was out killing a chicken to dress. He knew she was missing the blue bead. He came running saying, "Look what I found!" He had found that glass bead in the chicken's gizzard. She washed the bead and strung it back on her necklace.

Addie Bleckley: One time we were spending Christmas Eve night at my grandmother's, and two of our aunts were there. Aunt Maggie went to town and bought a doll for my older sister, Myrt, but never got me anything. It came time to hang up the stockings, and my other aunt realized she didn't have anything for me. So she got on a horse and rode to town and got me a doll like Myrt's. I was pretty small, but I was old enough to play with a doll, and I didn't have one. I won't ever forget her for that. She made me a very happy little girl.

Jim Tipton: Anna Tipton, my mother, used to live in an orphanage. A little drum was her favorite gift. The orphanage would not let people take the orphans home for Christmas, so they took them before Christmas. The people who took her had another girl her age. The girl showed her

around the store. She did not know the people were following her. The girl told what she liked, and Anna told what
she liked. They looked at about twelve things. When Christmas came, there were about twelve things under the Christmas tree. She was so surprised, because they were exactly
the things she liked. The people who took her to their
house got them for her.

Shane Chadwell: Living in Richmond as a little boy, I
always wanted a dog. So one day my dad walked in the
kitchen with a box in his hands and told me to open it.
Taking the box from his strong, sturdy hands, I set it on
the ground. I pulled the string on the box, and there was a
head covered in fur that popped out. Whimpering and
crying before me was a little German shepherd puppy that
belonged to me and no one else but me.

I grew more and more fond of the puppy each day. I
soon got tired of calling him "dog," so I came up with
"Brownie." Growing so fond of Brownie, I started getting
Mom and Dad to buy Christmas presents for him. Every
Christmas just kept getting better and better because Brownie
got smarter, and I grew fonder of him.

There was one Christmas which I remember was my
worst Christmas. It was snowing really hard. Snowflakes
were like falling stars from the sky, and I let Brownie out
to use the bathroom. After awhile I went back out to get
him, and he was gone. A trail of blood led from where he
had been to the woods. I ran into the house crying and
screaming for Mom to help me. She came running and
said, "What's the matter?" I told her that I had gone to get
Brownie and had found a trail of blood going to the woods.
When Dad got home from work, we followed the trail

of blood into the woods. After hours of searching we found Brownie laying on his side with my neighbor standing over him. My neighbor said that a wolf was killing his chickens. Brownie had killed one of his chickens and carried it into the woods; my neighbor saw him and thought he was the wolf. Instead of checking, he shot Brownie. It took me a long time to get over Brownie because Christmas is a time for giving, not taking.

Brent Brown: I asked my grandmother [Doris Andrews] about her most memorable Christmas. She told me about one when she was eleven years old. Her father had lost his job and they were very poor. She didn't think she would get anything, and she felt awful. She woke up on Christmas Day, and under the tree there was a peppermint stick that was hers. That was her most memorable Christmas because her parents couldn't afford it at the time.

Louise Hooper: The Christmas that really comes to mind is the year that my daddy was out of work. It was kind of a sad Christmas because there was no money for gifts. All we got that Christmas was a tiny container of candy, the kind people use now to decorate cookies and cakes with. The thing that bothered my sister and me was that we both knew how hurt our parents were that they couldn't buy us anything.

Clyde Hodge: I remember my fifth Christmas. We lived about ten miles up in a holler. People couldn't travel in the holler except by walking. My daddy worked in the coal mines. There were eleven of us. We lived in a two-room shack. We never hardly had anything to eat, but all the other little neighbor kids said, "Christmas is coming!

Christmas is coming! We're going to get something!" We didn't know what Christmas was, but we got caught up in the excitement. We really thought we were going to get something. Mom said we could [each] put up a Christmas tree, so all of my brothers and sisters began looking for our own Christmas tree. I picked a small cedar tree. My older brother helped nail it on a stake for me. I put it beside the bed and decorated it with pieces of stuff I found around the house such as pieces of cloth and tin foil. There was anticipation in our hearts because of this great day. I didn't know what Christmas meant or who Santa was, but everybody was excited. You know how a little child gets all caught up in the adventure.

Well, the big day arrived. We got up that morning and walked in, looked under our little trees! There was nothing, absolutely nothing! I thought, "Why were all the kids excited? There's nothing under my tree! I thought something must have happened, maybe Santa lost our presents!

Then I remembered they said Santa Claus wouldn't come to a house if you are mean. I thought, "Well, I must have been a mean boy." I made up my mind I wasn't going to be mean anymore.

Then I went over to the neighbor's house to find out if Santa had passed them by, too. Of course, I knew they had been meaner than me, but to my surprise Santa had stopped at their house. You can't imagine my astonishment when the little girl brought out the prettiest little doll you ever did see, and the little boy had the fanciest cap pistol I had ever seen. He shot bang! bang! bang! I couldn't understand why Santa Claus stopped there. They were mean kids. But they still received gifts! Why not me?

That Christmas came up a big disappointment. I cried

161

because I couldn't understand. But I thought next year things were going to be different. Santa will stop at our house. But I met with disappointments the next year and the next year also.

After that when I was about nine, I was so depressed because when I went to school everybody looked forward to Christmas. They wrote letters to Santa asking for presents. So I wrote one too. Maybe this was what I had been doing wrong all these years. I had forgot to write to Santa and tell him what I wanted and where I lived.

At school, the teacher asked, "Have you been good this year?"

I said, "Yes, I've been so good."

I just knew this year Santa would make it to my house! This Christmas morning, I woke up before anyone else did. I said to myself, "I want to see what I got. I've been so good this year."

To my amazement, there was nothing under the tree, not one thing! I checked all nine trees and there was nothing. I was so sad, I cried again. All the other children at school had told us about the great Christmas dinner they had last year. Dinnertime arrived and to my surprise it was not special, but the same water gravy and biscuits that we had every day. Christmas was a big disappointment. I couldn't understand; everybody else was making such a big deal over Christmas.

I went next door to see little Susie. I wanted to know if Santa had stopped at her house again this year.

Susie answered the door and said, "Oh, Clyde, look what I got for Christmas."

She had the most beautiful blond-headed doll I had ever seen.

I stammered, "It is a beautiful doll, Susie."

But my thoughts flashed, why had Susie got something for Christmas and I never got anything? I made up my mind that it was not fair that Susie got a doll and I didn't get anything. I waited patiently for Susie to lay down her new doll. We played for an hour. Then Susie's mother called her to dinner.

I said, "Let me hold your baby while you eat."

Susie said, "You can hold her until I get back."

Quick as Susie went to the house, I took off with the dollie. I thought if I couldn't get anything from Santa, Susie would have to forfeit her doll, too. I climbed up on this big rock cliff in the backyard. I found a hole under this boulder. I took her doll and hid it. Then I piled rocks over the hole to cover it up. I sneaked down from the cliff and went in the house. I sat down on the floor appearing to be busy.

Susie began hollering, "Clyde, where's my dollie? Clyde, where's my dollie? Where's my dollie?"

I said, "Somebody must have stolen your dollie."

She ran home crying, "Momma, Momma, someone stole my dollie."

Well, you probably guessed, her momma marched over and asked, "Where's Susie's dollie?"

I said, "I don't know where Susie's dollie is."

But when Dad came home and took me out back to the shed and used his belt, I confessed to burying her doll. I laid in my bed thinking that night what Christmas is all about. How exciting it is to get the whipping of your life. It's not worth it, but I was optimistic. Maybe something wonderful would happen. Each year it got a little harder to bear. Until I was twelve years old, I thought Christmas was all going to be alike!

But this Christmas my oldest sister got married and moved to Ohio. She came to visit. We put up our traditional nine Christmas trees. I will never be able to explain my surprise when I got up that Christmas morning. There was a package under my tree! The first time it had ever happened to me! I was stunned! I just stared at the present. It had my name written on a piece of paper.

My sister said, "Clyde, aren't you going to open the gift?"

Finally, I opened the package, and to my delight it was a Ben Casey shirt! The biggest thing in the whole school was a Ben Casey shirt. Everyone had been watching the Ben Casey show and he was our hero.

I had to tell Susie and every neighbor in the holler that I had gotten a Ben Casey shirt. This was my prized possession. I wore that Ben Casey shirt until it fell off. I would not take it off. I slept in it, I ate in it, I wore it every day, seven days a week, until it finally fell in a rag. They couldn't get it off of me. The only way it got washed was when I took a bath in the creek.

The next Christmas I expected another since my brothers got married, but I didn't get a gift. They brought us apples and oranges. This was a treat because usually our meals consisted of water gravy and biscuits for breakfast. For dinner, we had cornmeal gravy and biscuits, and for supper there was water gravy and biscuits. Sometimes we had rabbit or squirrel if one of us boys were lucky enough to kill one. Fruit was an unexpected blessing for us.

Through my high school days, we still continued to put up our separate trees, expecting something. I thought less and less of this great day.

When I married, I guess I expected the same old

thing—disappointment. But instead, it was the best of my life, all because my wife taught me what Christmas was all about. She taught me that Jesus was born and we were celebrating Jesus' birth.

Now since I am older, I finally understand why Santa Claus couldn't find our holler. I realize that my mom and dad never had any money. Food was the most important thing, and we usually never had enough to completely fill us up!

To many people today, that Ben Casey shirt wouldn't have meant much, but we all wore flour-sack dresses. Boys and girls alike. A store-bought shirt was something that we never had until we were old enough to work in the coal mines or tobacco fields. We wore hand-me-down clothes, passed from child to child. By the time nine children had wore the clothes, there wasn't much left but holes and patches.

As a child, Christmas didn't have a meaning to all of us kids. When I married and found out the real meaning of Christmas, it not only erased the old sorrows and disappointments, but I found out about true happiness. Jesus came to bring us life. That is the least anyone could have in this world today.

I had always dreamed of a great Christmas just like in the story books. The Lord gave me a fantastic one with my wife. When we sat down to dinner and we blessed the food, I had to thank the Lord again. The table sported a big twenty-eight-pound turkey, plus dressing, sweet potatoes, gravy, rolls, pies, and cakes. I thought, Lord, this can't be real! It was like a picture in a fairytale. This day I could eat until I wasn't hungry!

Student Authors and Interviewees

(CHS) = Corbin High School, Corbin, Kentucky
(HTES) = Hightower Trail Elementary School, Conyers, Georgia
(MES) = Maynardville Elementary School, Maynardville, Tennessee
(MEHS) = Morristown East High School, Morristown, Tennessee
(RCHS) = Rabun County High School, Rabun County, Georgia
(RGNS) = Rabun Gap-Nacoochee School, Rabun Gap, Georgia
(RHS) = Rockcastle County High School, Mount Vernon, Kentucky
(RSES) = Rush Strong Elementary School, Strawberry Plains, Tennessee
(SCHS) = Stephens County High School, Toccoa, Georgia
(TES) = Thrasher Elementary School, Signal Mountain, Tennessee

The list that follows gives the name of each person interviewed, the person(s) who conducted the interview, and the school the interviewer(s) attends. Thus the first item on the list can be explained in this manner: The interview with Doris Andrews was conducted by Brent Brown, a student of Stephens County High School. In places where only one name appears on a line, an interview was not involved. Rather a student did it from memory.

Andrews, Doris, by Brent Brown (SCHS)
Barron, Vadie, by Stacy Barron (RHS)
Bleckley, Addie, by Suzanne Hassell and Libbi Burney
Bradley, Ruthie
Bradshaw, Burice, by Nicole Edwards (RCHS)
Brooks, Florence, by Rebecca Hill and Julia Justice (RCHS)
Brooks, Lawton, by Richard Edwards (RCHS)
Brown, Mrs. E. H., by Anita Hamilton, Kaye Carver, and Maybelle
     Carpenter (RCHS)
Brown, Marinda
Brown, Maude, by Beth Ray (RGNS)
Brumett, Delsie, by Christy Brumett (RHS)
Bulgin, John, by Allison Adams, Mark Edwards, Joseph Fowler,
     and Kelly Shropshire (RCHS)
Bulgin, Margaret, by Allison Adams, Mark Edwards, Joseph Fowler
     and Kelly Shropshire (RCHS)
Campbell, Nola, by Allison Adams and OhSoon Shropshire (RCHS)
Cannon, Aunt Lola, by Myra Queen and Anita Jenkins (RCHS)
Cannon, Edith, by Scott Cannon and Chris Nix (RCHS)
Cannon, Robert, by Scott Cannon and Chris Nix (RCHS)
Carver, Emma Sue, by Jason Boggs (CHS)
Carver, Leona, by Robbie Bailey and Anthony Queen (RCHS)
Chadwell, Shane (RHS)
Coggins, Lora, by Julie Dickens (RCHS)
Coldren, Louise, by Rabun Baldwin, John Crane, and Keri Gragg
     (RCHS)
Conner, Lessie, by Joseph Fowler and Kelly Shropshire (RCHS)
Conner, Minyard, by Joseph Fowler and Kelly Shropshire (RCHS)
Corn, Ethel, by Anita Hamilton, Kaye Carver, and Maybelle Car-
     penter (RGNS)
Cranwell, Susan, by Beth Cranwell (TES)
Cromer, Wanda, by Julian Cromer (RHS)
Crone, Ada, by Carol Ramey (RCHS)

Lusk, Alma, by Mark Edwards, Joseph Fowler, and Robin Lakey (RCHS)
McCall, Lassie, by Richard Edwards and Donna Ramey (RCHS)
McCurry, Gail, by Lori McCurry (TES)
McDaries, Mary, by Paula Mahan (CHS)
McGaha, Mattie Pearl, by Bruce Beck, Allison Bethel, Beth Davis, Julie Dickens, Shannon Edwards, Jena Kelly, Jenny Lincoln, Susan Shirley, Joey Steill (RCHS)
McWherter, Hazel Duvall, by Bruce Beck, Allison Bethel, Beth Davis, Julie Dickens, Shannon Edwards, Jena Kelly, Jenny Lincoln, Susan Shirley, Joey Steill (RCHS)
Miller, Barbara, by Aaron Miller (HTES)
Neal, Ida, by Deidre Stubblefield (MEHS)
Norton, Addie, by Claire Bender, Laurie Brunson, Debbie Crowell, Karen Moore, Juli Pankey, and Sensi Sise (RGNS)
Norton, Aunt Mo and Tommy Lee, by Renai Crane, Tammi English, and Holli Hickox (RCHS)
Parker, Eula, by Bruce Beck (RCHS)
Patterson, Burma, by Donna Ramsey and Richard Edwards (RCHS)
Patterson, Iris
Perry, Annie, by Beverly Justice (RGNS)
Pitts, Mary, by Bruce Beck (RCHS)
Ponder, Elmer, by Jennifer Rogers (RHS)
Ponder, Lucille, by Jennifer Rogers (RHS)
Proffitt, Missi, by Diane Mitchell (CHS)
Reynolds, Virginia Gail, by Jenny Lovell (RHS)
Ricker, Doris, by Robert Ricker (MEHS)
Rickman, Icie, by Chuck Clay and Rob Stockton (RCHS)
Robertson, Bill, by Victoria Singleton (RHS)
Rubel, Edwina, by Tim Rubel (RCHS)
Runion, Clyde, by Caney English, Roger Little, and Dale Trusty (RCHS)
Shumate, Doris, by Raymond McDonnell (MES)
Skeen, Lula, by Nicole Skeen (MEHS)
Stiner, Lilian, by Cathy Wallace (RCHS)
Stradley, Carolyn, by Allison Adams, Eddie Kelly, and Patsy Singleton (RCHS)
Stubblefield, J. C., by Sharon Gravley (RCHS)
Taylor, Bernice, by Sharon Gravley (RCHS)

Taylor, Janie P., by Allison Bethel, Shay Daniels, Julie Dickens, and Shelly Hunnicutt (RCHS)
Thurmond, Annie, by Teresa Thurmond (RCHS)
Thurston, Juanita, by Kevin Ledford (CHS)
Tipton, Anna, by Jim Tipton (RSES)
Toothman, Lyndall "Granny", by Kim Baldwin, Clark Bowen, Kevin Cannon, and Richard Harmon (RCHS)
Tudor, Marie, by Carol Whitney (RSES)
Van Winkle, Janet (RHS)
Vanzant, Judy, by Everett Lee Vanzant (CHS)
Whiten, Lutrelle, by Jennifer McDougal (SCHS)
Wigington, Christine, by Mark Turpen, OhSoon Shropshire, Dawn Watson, and Richard Edwards (RCHS)
Williams, Bernice, by Nicole Edwards (RCHS)
Wilson, Pauline, by Jill Martin (MEHS)

With special thanks to Sarah Connelly Reed for help with the recipes

🔆 **Eliot Wigginton,** who started *Foxfire* magazine with his ninth- and tenth-grade English classes in 1966, still teaches high school in the Appalachian Mountains of North Georgia and, with his students, guides the activities of The Foxfire Fund, Inc. Mr. Wigginton has just won a MacArthur Foundation Fellowship for his work in public education.